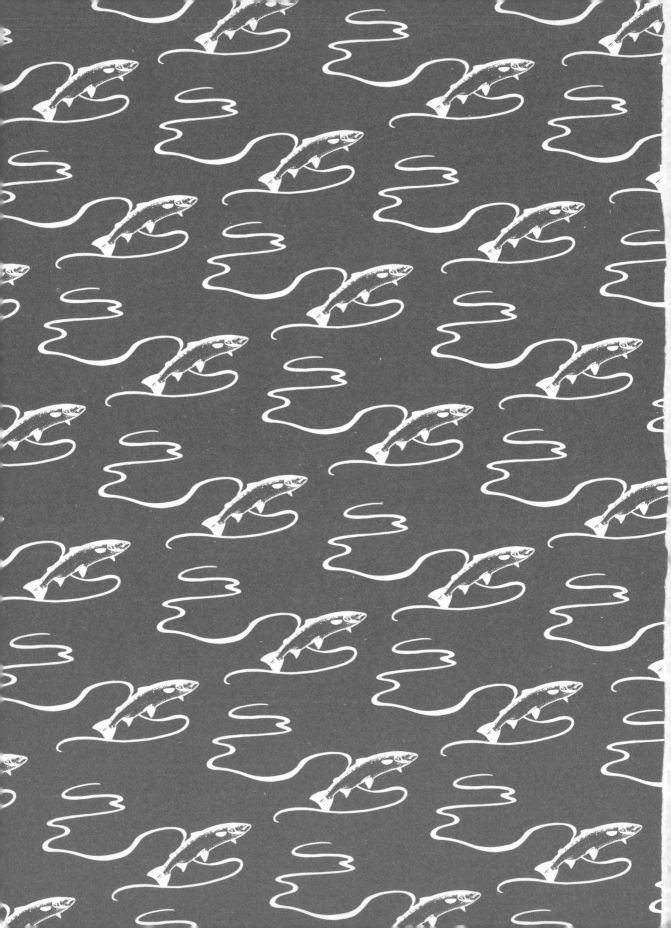

Salar the Salmon

Henry watching for salmon at Sloping Weir. Photographed about the time of writing 'Salar'. He is wearing the leather coat worn for fast journeys in his Alvis sports car.

THE ILLUSTRATED

Salar the Salmon

HENRY WILLIAMSON

Introduction by Richard Williamson

With illustrations and a Foreword by Michael Loates

David R. Godine, Publisher · BOSTON

To
T. E. LAWRENCE
of
Seven Pillars of Wisdom
and
V. M. YEATES
of
Winged Victory

Published in 1990 by
David R. Godine, Publisher, Inc.
Horticultural Hall
300 Massachusetts Avenue
Boston, Massachusetts 02115

Library of Congress Catalog Card Number: 89-46181
ISBN: 0-87923-845-3

First published by the author in 1935
This edition first published in Great Britain by Webb & Bower (Publishers) Limited 1987
5 Cathedral Close, Exeter, Devon EX1 1EZ in association with
Michael Joseph Limited
27 Wrights Lane, London W8 5TZ
by arrangement with Faber & Faber

First printing
Printed in Hong Kong

Contents

Contents

Foreword

I have no qualms about stating that my greatest moving influence in life has been the writings of Henry Williamson. Here was a man who had put into words that which I felt but had no ability to express; whose prose described the visions in my head. It struck me as no small coincidence that his domestic life and early years up to the Great War had run such a similar course to my own; an inevitable fascination followed.

Wanderings and fishing days for me began at 'Ceasar's Well', Keston Ponds. Norman's Park, Bromley Common, Holwood Park and the infant River Ravensbourne were all places I knew intimately, now sadly swallowed-up within the spreading brick and mortar of Greater London. With bicycle and increasing wanderlust I was drawn further afield to Squerryes Park and the Darenth Valley. All these places Henry knew some fifty years before I did. Later, in my first car, I journeyed to Devon and found a landscape that was wild and free, and, in youthful aloneness, gave rise to all hope and dream. At that time I was 'serving sentence' in the London advertising world and loathing it. I felt stifled with much to say but no way of expressing it. Throughout that fruitless time Henry's words were hope. I was warned, I would outgrow this obsession, but I never did and now, some fifteen years on, Henry still remains my departed 'soul brother' as he himself described Richard Jefferies, his own great influence.

During the illustrating of this volume I spent several days, armed with sketchpad and camera, walking the banks of the Taw, Mole and Bray. It would have been easy to become awe-struck by the grandeur of the riverscape but, as Henry had done, I entered into the environs of fish by isolating the smaller details of the salmon's world. I studied individual stones and gravel and made many drawings of bankside foliage and, of ultimate importance, made acute observation of the visual rhythms of water with its varying light play. Throughout the summer, autumn and winter I watched salmon and sea trout ascending my own river in South Devon. I saw silver schools, fresh in from their ocean voyage running the tidal pools of the estuary. Following their course upriver to the foot of Dartmoor I saw them leaping in times of spate, sulking in low, clear water and their silver sea lustre slowly turn to red with spawning fever. Finally, on the last day of January after the snows had melted away, I walked upriver to make observations for the book's finale. The water was low and running gin clear with only the notes of the dipper and the river's song breaking the wintry silence. There, lying in the shallow margins I found a kelt, its spent form covered in fungus, waiting for the rains to take the wasted body seawards over the gravels of its birth. In this eerie silence I peered into deep, cold blue pools. They seemed empty, devoid of life; an impenetrable world that quietly held a death sentence for the majestic fish. Yet one knew, in that seemingly alien world beneath the boulders and within the gravel beds, alevin were stirring, awaiting the spring sunlight. I walked homewards with an emotional vision firmly implanted and set to work painting the plate for the final chapter.

Where possible I have interpreted Henry's words faithfully, although in some instances the composition of the painting meant that certain features would have been a distraction to the main subject. For instance, in the painting of 'Old Nog' perched on an oak post peering low for fish I could have included three swans and the flock of shelduck, even a boat or two. However, I felt the painting was about atmosphere, the siting of the heron and the oak posts. Further elements would have been unnecessary distractions to those main features.

Some fifty years after the books first publication one is acutely aware that the Atlantic salmons' status is tragically far removed from the great runs of Salar's day. Indeed, the plates in this book represent a dying world. Ironically, the day I visited the 'Junction Pool' there, beneath the bank at the confluence of Taw and Mole, was a poacher's net with a snared cock salmon visibly gasping its last. During those wanderings along Taw, Mole and Bray I did see some salmon and a fair number of peal (sea trout). From the parapet of Humpy Bridge, Shallowford, I gazed down into the deep pool beneath catching sight of several large fish. There, too, were the dippers and grey wagtails dancing and singing on the gravelly margins – and 'Old Nog' was forever appearing along my journey. Perhaps it was not all a sad case for melancholic reflection.

Although Henry found the writing of 'Salar' difficult and sometimes tedious, it has nothing less of the dedication and sensitivity of 'Tarka'. The harsh reality of the natural world is all here; no sentimentality. He again strived for that never-attainable state of perfection in his work as I have tried to achieve in the paintings. We never reach that perfect state and perhaps it is this very frustration that motivates further work.

Henry sometimes saw his own life as a salmon whose mysterious lifestyle runs an endless gauntlet of predation to ultimate tragedy. He was a 'water-spirit' whose thoughts flowed as his own River Bray, singing over sun-dappled gravel in springtime to the swirling turmoil of autumn's silty spates. I believe that both Tarka and Salar were personal statements. They were a part of Henry.

Here then is my own visual statement which I like to think would have pleased Henry as his own work has pleased and inspired me. I am privileged indeed to have contributed to such an outstanding literary classic.

The Paintings & Drawings

When I undertook to illustrate this new edition of *Salar the Salmon* my prime consideration was that the work should compliment a literary classic by a literary genius. I didn't, therefore, think in terms of here today, gone tomorrow illustrations, but chose to treat each plate as a painting drawn from the same visions which had fired the author all those years ago.

Each painting has been produced on a white, hand-made Hayle Mill paper and treated in transparent watercolour over a rigorous and thorough pencil drawing. This provides a strong visual base thus enabling one to minimise the use of excessive colour. All whites and light areas are from the paper itself, (with the exception of the stars on page 42). The artist's insistence, rightly or wrongly, to totally avoid the use of white paint or body colour, stems from an almost masochistic challenge. I see little, if any point in painting anything which one feels will come easily. Each work must be a highly disciplined exercise, throughout whose execution there should, for me, be a hesitancy bordering on fear of ruining the picture. On completion the quality and aesthetic value of the painting should be that much greater for this discipline.

Whilst the works may look detailed, this was not paramount in my thinking. What I was concerned with was atmosphere, quality of light and overcoming the problems beset me without the work becoming laboured. The full page originals were painted 17ins × 12¼ins and the half pages 9ins × 12¼ins, thus reduction gives a greater sense of detail.

Throughout the paintings the smallest brush used was a No4 WN series 7 with much of the work carried out in dry-brush. The pencil drawings were all completed with HB and B pencils.

Although the illustrations in their entirety took little more than six months to produce, the visions and knowledge of the subject stem from a lifetime's water-watching and observation in the field.

Mick Loates
Kingsbridge, S. Devon

Introduction

After the success of *Tarka the Otter*, which took the reading world by storm and awarded the author The Hawthornden Prize in 1928, a similar style of book was commissioned in 1933. My father, Henry Williamson, was thirty-seven years of age, and needed the money. There were three children to feed and another on the way, as well as a secretary, house-keeper and gardener to pay. He had written fifteen books and many articles for newspapers and magazines as well as broadcasts for the BBC. But he had expensive tastes – a sports car, a London club, good clothes, and private fishing.

The commission came from the publishing firm of Faber and Faber, one of whose directors, Dick De la Mare, son of the poet Walter, had been my father's best man eight years before. To keep the family afloat he had paid for the salmon book long before pen had been put to paper. It was a courageous decision; he had had to persuade the other directors to back him and the investment needed a sale of ten thousand copies to repay. But this was in the days of 'gentlemen publishers' who were as much patrons of the arts as the wealthy aristocrats of previous centuries. Without De la Mare, quite possibly this book would not have been written.

Salar, which is a latin word meaning leaper, is the story of a salmon in a compelling world of colour and drama. A fisherman will tell you that the facts are correct and match his own knowledge of what goes on beneath the water. However, many are the wildlife stories that are correct in fact and alive with adventure; what is rare is to find one that is also poetically satisfying, allowing us to experience those feelings we thought too private to admit, perhaps being too close to tears or exposing too great a desire for beauty.

Salar is a book that began by representing the yearnings, both physical and spiritual, for a young woman, whom I shall not name because she is still alive. From his diaries it is evident that my father was in some torment. In her he imagined that he had at last found the perfect partner, who felt exactly as he did, who sympathised with his needs and was able, with unusual self confidence for a sixteen year old, to counter his damaging feelings of self pity and incipient cruelty to those who loved him. Very quickly he began to spin her bridal veil of fantasy, adding where she showed promise, hiding where she was lacking, arranging and decorating her for what he hoped would be the eventual and long awaited spiritual and physical ceremony. That he had courted these will o' the wisps before was forgotten. There were one or two drawbacks, one being the disapproval of the girl's parents, with whom we may commiserate. But to my father, this was a personal affront. It is difficult for us to understand his feelings; the poet's intense feeling and vision for his creation, which is much more real and vivid to him than real life and is protected with a jealous zeal knowing no social boundaries. In his deeply intimate diary he records '. . . wrote her a letter, which like its kind, did not and shall not post. Too poetical, too sad-feeling. This repels the living. Its incommunicable, unshareable feeling.' Later he recorded, at the height of this relationship: '. . . she is a spirit of . . . inspiration, a celestial parthenon, a bright visitant from the sky . . . sometimes I feel it can never be, that it is an illusion, the old error of the search for the gold falcon outside one's half ruined self'. It was an illusion of the physical world that he had dreaded since childhood, and its translation into the spiritual or artistic was the only method of capture. Little wonder that, in fear and terror of losing the new image, he wrote to the girl's father: 'You are destroying my imagination', although the protective parent could only have been bewildered at this statement.

In order to retain the image, he sketched out, desperately one senses, the crude basis for this story: salmon = poet's soul = girl; fisherman = girl's father.

The physical relationship did not materialise, but the slow-burning spiritual fuse had been lit and the girl began gradually to drop away, her part expended, like the first stage of a rocket. Throughout his writing career it is obvious, perhaps more to the observer than to my father, that many women played these vital roles. My mother had been partly the genesis for the famous *Flax of Dream* novels which had made his name in the 1920s, and she appeared and reappeared throughout later novels with reliable regularity. Despite the girl-friends, he remained married to her for twenty-four years and had an unwavering respect and trust for her all his life. But she had a difficult life, never knowing when he would reappear or with whom; she usually had to put up with the frayed edge of life.

Little of this was evident to the children, although my brother John has said how he would hear, and be troubled by, the cries of misery from the writing room as the self-doomed writer struggled to contact his Muse and so quell the riot of hobgoblins representing failures, errors and misunderstandings. Often we children played in the river with our father, moving rocks around to redirect the flow, dragging out branches for firewood washed down in winter spates, feeding the pet trout and salmon which lived in the pool below Humpy Bridge and bathing there in summertime when the meadows were cropped like fine lawns by dairy cattle whose tails swished the buttercups. Either side of the valley towered two hills with their dense pine woods where buzzards nested and wheeled forth onto the air currents for play, circling higher and higher into cloud. From a tunnel inside the hill a train would hourly burst with a flag of steam, to clank high above the valley on its viaduct, as suddenly to vanish. It was exciting to climb there, and listen for the tremor of iron wheels a mile away and imagine the horror of jumping from the rails in the nick of time.

This was my father's play area too. He had a mile of fishing and spent much of his time in the water, experimenting with different rods, reels and artificial flies, hoping against hope one day to achieve the climax of four years of river watching, the capture of an Atlantic salmon. As I write this I have his Pandora's box of gear and tackle beside me, made of mahogany with a lid and drawer lined with finest green velvet. It has probably not been touched for forty years. There are dozens of lacquered swivels and stainless steel hooks, brass spinners, an aluminium gut-cast box with an embossed salmon on the lid, a miniature corked bottle of fly dressing and midge repellent, a small box of dapping hooks, scores of lead weights and a box containing 'Charley's Crawfish Crawler' from America. Then there are the little boxes with artificial flies of every hue, still hooked to their nickel plated catches or nestling inside miniature mica lidded containers; turquoise, gold, red and amber, the feathers of birds from every corner of the world. Also packets of Hercules single gut traces, semi-invisible patent stain 'soak them longer they are stronger', the 'red loop' casts from Milward-Bartleet of Redditch, the 'Test' casts from Ogden Smiths of Piccadilly, dry fly wallets by Charles Farlow of The Strand, and of course the superb fly rods. The first of these by Parker Hale and the second, a greenheart split cane made and signed by John Lames Hardy, the 'Palakona', No 246396, encased in its polished aluminium tube and wrapped inside a cloth sleeve lest the tip, no thicker than a damselfly's body, be broken by clumsy fingers. As children we were hardly allowed to look at it or breathe on it, never mind touch it; it was practically an icon. Dressed in special tweeds, plus fours and jacket, tie and hat, my father would find solace in the rushing waters and dimpled pools of the Bray, seeking the unattainable; to catch for ever his maiden salmon.

As he fished he watched, marked, and noted down everything that he saw. He had learned as an Army officer to record everything. In the trenches he had been in command of a supply outpost up the lines, and had made daily records, keeping the carbon copies for later use in his war novels. For the writing of *Tarka* he had noted details of every bend, pool and tree of the rivers where he sought his story. Now the notebook was used again, as today a writer would use a tape-recorder, except that diagrams and cartoons showed details such as water direction and speed, build up of gravel, position of trees and bankside flowers. The *Encyclopaedia Britannica* was consulted several times, so were the *Salmon & Trout* magazines.

He also rigged up an old aquarium on the writing room table, fed by well water, to watch the behaviour of newly hatched fish. Out in the meadow a small hatchery was built, and there he would lie for hours watching the fry growing to parr, seeing them station themselves and hover in the water waiting for food, understanding their needs and moods and all their dynamics, as a scientist would observe the behaviour of a new aircraft in a wind tunnel. Accuracy was essential, not just for the satisfaction of receiving the approbation of fellow fishermen – which would include Lord Fortescue, the owner of his house, the river, and the surrounding landscape – but more importantly the gratification that he had been true and faithful to his talent, what he called the life force, in whose way nothing was allowed to stand. He had a personal need to understand and illustrate divine creation, which was truth and love.

The salmon, lying in crystal surroundings, of perfect aquadynamic shape, struggling through continual hazards and against a thousand slings and arrows to achieve the holiest of ideals, the continuation of the species, was a creature to be revered, one with whose troubles he could easily identify. In his book, *A Clearwater Stream* published twenty years later, he described salmon as noble and tragic, like soldiers in battle, in the test to destruction, upheld only by a tenuous dream which was honour. No wonder that he began the book with a quote from William Blake on the title page: 'Everything that lives is holy', although this was later erased.

During 1934 my father wrote two books to keep the pot boiling. The first was a series of forty essays collectively entitled *The Linhay on the Downs*, and the second was *Devon Holiday* at which he worked for twelve hours a day, sometimes completing fifteen thousand words a day, and finishing it in only a month.

On October 8th he hooked a salmon, which was played for half an hour before finally landing. So excited was he that he telegraphed to Charles Tunnicliffe, who had illustrated his books before, and the artist travelled all night arriving at 9.39 the next morning. For four days the two walked and watched the river, the dead salmon was sketched and photographed and then '. . . Tunny left, having many terrific ideas and sketches.' But the euphoria faded away again as winter began, boredom and listlessness set in and he had

Top Left:
The author with the salmon taken at Humpy Bridge, Shallowford.

Top Right:
Salmon leaping at Sloping Weir, photographed by the author.

Above:
The Fireplay Pool in summer, with John the author's son.

Centre:
Henry about to take the plunge into Humpy Bridge Pool.

Right:
The author's wife, Loetitia, and their son John, hold the salmon caught at Humpy Bridge.

pains in his back 'as though an assegai point were stuck between two of my spinal sections'. So the winter dragged, he did little writing; guilt at receiving the advance for *Salar* in October manifesting itself by petty squabbles in the home. It was not until the New Year of 1935, and the returning pendulum of the sun to the dark little valley, that things began at last to happen and the imagination had lift off.

'Jan. 23rd. Played badminton at South Molton last night, enjoyable, sweated some, and on returning tubbed and changed, felt clear and fine and began about 7.15 pm *Atlantic Salmon*.' It was two years since the first offer by the publishers, and three months since the first payment. The writing progressed at about seven hundred words a day, and on the second day the title was changed to *Salar the Leaper*. After that there were few diary entries. One, five months before I was born, announced 'My wife is apparently going to present herself with another infant . . . young Master Richard will make his debut in August'. The other entries were that his father-in-law died (the old man had been portrayed in previous books and was admired for his courteous good manners), that George 5th's Jubilee was celebrated on May 6th when the family had a bonfire, one of twenty-seven on surrounding hills, and that Lawrence of Arabia was killed on his motorcycle having driven to Bovington Camp to telegraph my father about a proposed meeting the next day. Thereafter the pages are blank. When not writing he was fishing or watching, often with a persistent influenza that would not get better and worried the local doctor who only saw his patient in bed during the five minutes when he called, not soaked to the skin wading in floods or sitting up a tree in the rain gathering material for the next chapter. My mother was often very worried; once he disappeared down the river for a whole day and half the night, returning soaked again having walked miles downstream.

A day or two after my birth, on August 5th, *Salar* was finished at the writing hut twenty miles from home near Georgeham. A fan who called on him a little before the end said he looked ghastly, white faced and unshaven, but greeted the fan, whom he had never seen before, with the words 'Come on in and have some lime juice, it wards off the skurvy'. He confessed that writing the book had been agony, much worse than *Tarka*, which had been rewritten seventeen times.

The chapters were sent off as they were completed, to be set up immediately and the book was on sale just over two months later in mid October. It had excellent reviews. Sixty-four newspapers or magazines discussed it, some at great length. There were almost no harsh nor doubtful words, but continual praise and wonder. The *Daily Mirror* said that it was written with uncanny insight into a world utterly remote from the life of man. *The Times Literary Supplement* thought that it was a searching and comprehensive life history which, for absorbing interest, left behind many a romance of human character. *The Observer* decided that river life was never more thrilling. A month later, when they saw how the book was catching on, they gave it another review, almost quarter of a page, when they discussed the whole business of science meeting art, an event that to this day remains quite rare. The *Daily Telegraph* thought it better than *Tarka*, while *The Financial Times* recommended it as excellent reading. Within a week it had to be reprinted, and it sold ten thousand copies before Christmas. The publisher's faith had paid off. With several children to feed the money was needed, but the author had himself paid a high price. His creation had gone, he was returned to the physical world to contemplate the next earthly attempt at spiritual apotheosis. Fortunately for us, there were to be many such attempts.

Richard Williamson

BOOK ONE

Book One: Tideways

1 Sea Assembly

At full moon the tides swirling over the Island Race carry the feelings of many rivers to the schools of fish which have come in from their feeding ledges of the deep Atlantic. The returning salmon are excited and confused. Under broken waters the moon's glimmer is opalescent; the fish swim up from ocean's bed and leap to meet the sparkling silver which lures and ever eludes them, and which startles them by its strange shape as they curve in air and see, during the moment of rest before falling, a thrilling liquescence of light on the waves beneath.

The Island Race is a meeting place of currents over a sunken reef, or chain of reefs. The sea is never still there. Twice every day and twice every night the tide rips over the ledges and pinnacles of the reef, streaming the seaweed under its white surges and mingling the layers of river waters in its green massive drifts.

Salmon feed in the Atlantic and return to the fresh-water rivers to spawn, and, by this arduous and pleasurable act, give of themselves to the immortality of salmon.

For two years after hatching the samlet lives and feeds in the river, and, having survived many dangers, drops down to the estuary in a new silver sea-coat, a slender little smolt no longer than a man's hand, bewildered and brave, entering with others of its school the thickening salt waters beyond the known river-water of its birth. It feels its way by the link of nerves, sensitive to the least pressure or density, along its sides from gill-covers to tail. The smolt, in its first armour of sea-scales, feeds eagerly on the new food moving in and stirring the sandy shore of ocean, shrimps and other small crustaceans and fish. In fresh-water life it was always head to stream, poised in eddy or by stone: thus it breathed through mouth and gill, thus it waited and watched for food moving or floating before and above its eyes, thus was it stream-tapered and made strong: a passing act in the everlasting action of its racial immortality. Always it was driving itself forward, to keep its poise, and its place in the stream.

In the sea it drove itself forward, a sideway sinuating movement, boring into the unknown and deepening densities of ocean. It found its new food more easily and frequently, it grew quickly, its shoulders deepened, its white flesh became pink, its forked tail-fin broadened. Always it was travelling farther from the shallow coast, yet following the weakening stream of fresh water beyond the last ribs of sand.

It came to a dark wall of rock from which ribbon weed was unrolling and swaying. The green water moved as in the river, but with greater press, and there the smolt waited in the race of tides, feeding on small fish which drifted past. Many smolts were taken by fish called bass, which, large mouthed and spined of back-fin, roved together down the corridors of the reef, and through the weedy timbers of wooden ships wedged in clefts of rock. The Island was a breeding place of sea birds, guillemots, auks, razorbills, puffins, red-throated divers, and others which oared themselves with their wings swiftly under water, while thrusting with webbed feet. Conger eels lived in dark water-caves, moving darkly and slowly behind broad-nosed heads, and suddenly accelerating along their own lengths to seize a fish before it could turn away. Loath to leave their remembered river-water, which was parent and friend to them, the smolts remained in a straggling school near the reef, among hundreds of thousands of other smolts, brought thither by their weakening parent streams.

The sun in Taurus rose over the land whose water-courses they had left, and set in the Atlantic; the tides poured over the reef, flowing north and lapsing south in light and darkness; the moon moved over the sea, and as its light grew so the tides pressed faster, mingling the river-streams until memory or feeling in the smolts for their rivers was lost in the greater movements of ocean. And in the night of the moon's fullness many shadows moved into the racing tide, and the smolts fled and gathered in confusion before the apparitions, which one after another swam slowly up to the broken, gleaming top of the sea and, near the surface, gathered all their power within themselves to sinuate first one side then the other, faster and faster gripping the water with one flank then the other to push their tapered lengths violently away from the water: thus a salmon accelerates for the leap. New schools of fish followed, slowly and leisurely, and ranged themselves behind and under and beside the salmon formations

already waiting in the tide-race. Fish after fish left its place, swam up, gathered strength, leapt, smacked down on its side, and swam down slowly to its place again.

The tide took the displaced smolts south of the Island, to where beyond rocks the water deepened and was quiet below the lift and roll of waves. So they began a far sea journey, their rivers disremembered. They wandered above rocky glooms of the deeper Atlantic; they wandered in ancestral memory. Here for many scores of thousands of years salmon had travelled, coming to where the last of the continent's foundations fell away into the blue twilight of immeasurable ocean.

In the sea was rich feeding; and when they were grown big, in surfeiture of physical life the unconscious lust for a fuller or spiritual life led them back along the undersea paths they had travelled as smolts, to where ancestral memory became personal memory – to where the river currents frayed away in the tidal rhythms of the sea. The returning salmon thinks with its whole body.

As the different schools found their food easily or hardly, so they grew quickly or slowly; thus salmon were returning to their rivers flowing into the North Atlantic at all months of the year, in varying tapers or sea-mouldings. Nevertheless, the salmon's cycle of renewal is fixed in the orbits of the sun, served by the moon; its spawning time is the end of the year, when days are short and rivers run high with wild rains. What of those fish which enter the rivers at the beginning of the year?

Should the early-running salmon survive the perils of the estuary, of river life in spring and summer, and endure the ardours of spawning and of prolonged starvation (for salmon feed only occasionally, and with no profit, in fresh water), it returns, sick and dislustred, to the sea, where, as fishermen say, it cleans itself; and again it journeys forth against the warm drag of the Gulf Stream with the eagerness of one reborn, yet who must follow the fixed orbit of its kind, unto that darkness which awaits even the sun in heaven. The scattered eggs of salmon in the gravel redds are as the constellations of night; nothing is lost of air or water. In this faith is the story of Atlantic salmon told.

The Romans, sailing their galleys between the Island and the mainland, knew the meeting place by the reef, and named the fish Salar—the Leaper. So shall be called the big keeper, or cock-fish, who sprang towards the moon from the waves of one of the biggest tides of the year on that coast, the Easter tide.

Salar was one of many thousands returning from the ocean feeding banks. As the moon at night rose fuller, he had travelled on, pausing neither to feed nor sleep. He had come at medium ocean cruising speed, travelling about a hundred miles from one sunrise to another, faster with the currents, slower aslant them. The current guided him; his body remembered. His mouth opened forty times every minute, and each time as his mouth closed his gill-covers opened, and red gill-rakers absorbed oxygen from the water for his blood-stream. In that blood-stream were units of life, even as the fish was a unit in the living sea.

Salar was five years old. During the two years of river life he had grown to a weight of two ounces: three years of ocean feeding had added another twenty pounds to his weight. Growth had not been regular or uniform. In two periods of sea wandering he, with other salmon, had increased rapidly, while following herring shoals on their westward migration after their spawning in the shallow waters of the north. The herring had followed drifting clouds of marine plankton, and salmon had pursued the herring shoals. Every day during these two periods Salar had gorged his own weight of herrings, catching a fish across the back as it turned from his upward rush, holding and crushing it in his jaws until it was dead, and then swallowing it head first. Soon his shoulders were hob-curved with stored power.

Pursuing the salmon were porpoises, led by Meerschwein, the old sea-hog. The porpoises hunted by swimming in formation under the salmon, which were under the herrings. They were invisible below. The only warning of Meerschwein's approach was a swirl and sudden varying water-pressure of the upward dash. He swam up under a salmon, gathered and launched himself at the fish, turned on his back and snapped at the salmon's belly. Meerschwein and the other porpoises fed by tearing away their bites; they seldom pursued a fish further. Like all carnivores, they had a sense of sport equal with the sense of feeding.

Following the porpoises were ferocious gladiators, or killers, led by Orca, the strongest, who could crush a porpoise with a single bite in the recurved teeth of his immense mouth. This tribe of killers, like the porpoises, were warm blooded, breathing only in air. They mated and brought forth their young under water. Their young were born with the instinct, or inherited custom, to inspire only when their mothers, to whom they clung, rolled on to the surface to breathe; but they could suck their dam's milk while submerged.

Salar had avoided death by bite of porpoise, shark, ray, and other predatory fish—nearly all fish prey on other fish—and now, five years and one month since hatching from a round egg about three-sixteenths of an inch in diameter in the head-waters of a stream under Snowdon, he was more than a yard long, and his girth was half his length.

He was lying on the edge of a current where it dragged against an eddy or back-trend of water; using one moving weight of water to buoy him against an opposing weight. He lolled there, at rest. He was nearly asleep. His mouth opened to take in water twenty times a minute.

Two lines of pierced scales along each flank covered cells filled with liquid which was sensitive to every varying pressure of moving water; the cells were joined with nerve-roots which connected with the brain. His body moved in idle flexion. Fins kept the body poised in its hover. On his back was the dorsal fin, behind each gill-cover was a pectoral fin. A little behind the point of the body's balance were the paired or ventral fins, by which he held himself when resting on a rock, or the bed of the sea in shallow water. By the caudal or tail fin he steered himself: a rudder. There was a small fixed fin, like a pennon, on his back, aft of the dorsal fin, which served to prevent turbulence or eddy when he was swimming forward. Blue and silver of flanks, porcelain white of belly, with fins of a delicate opaque greyish-pink, with a few yellow-red and grey-green and light brown spots on his gill-covers, and groups of sea-lice under the dark edge of his tail and on his back, Salar was resting in one of the many streaming currents at the eastern edge of the Island Race when Jarrk swam down, driving himself by powerful flippers, peering round and below with grey-filmy eyes. The seal scattered a school of grilse which flickered and flashed away in the tide. The sudden contorted beat of Salar as he accelerated thrummed in the seal's ears.

2 *Reef of Seals*

During the time of one wave-crest breaking white and reforming again in phosphoric streaks, nearly a thousand salmon which were resting in the tail of the Island Race had broken formation and were zigzagging into the northerly sweep of the tide. Many schools had been hovering there in echelon, bound for their various rivers—very large springers, five- and six-year-old fish; smaller spring fish with between two and three years of sea feeding; mended kelts—spawned fish which had "cleaned themselves" after spawning—the few survivors of the autumn run, biggest of the year, the authentic spawning run of salmon. The mended kelts would return along the way they had travelled as smolts.

A few of the schools were grilse, small fish which had been less than a year in salt water, weighing from three to eight pounds, slender, silver-grey, unspotted except faintly on gill-covers, with forked tail-fins and gracile "wrists"—the slender part of the body where it splayed into the tail-fin. One of the grilse, of a school of eleven which had been skittering along the moonlit surface and sporting among the wave-crests, was Gralaks, a young maiden salmon who had been born in one of the streams running down from the moor of the wild red deer, in the gravel redds above the pool called Fireplay.

Salar was a fish of the largest salmon river of that coast; he had hatched in one of its many head-waters breaking out of the slopes of Welsh mountains.

Salar saw Jarrk the seal as a luminous shape above him. An instant before he had shot away, the salmon had become alert because the seal's descent had altered the weight of one of the currents maintaining his lie. Jarrk's smooth hide reflected the broken confusion of light which was the surface of the sea, and when the seal had turned, his neck had flashed. Bubbles from his nostrils shone pearly.

Salar was away, the fish behind and beside him were away, and the alarm thudded through the sea, felt by the resting salmon above the pressure-roar of the currents.

Other seals were hunting the fish. Among them was a white seal which was followed by a baby seal four months old. The white seal lived on the rocks of Rat Isle, lying off the south-eastern corner of the Island and the home of the black rat, extinct on the mainland. The black rats had come there centuries before on a pirate's ship.

The baby seal when born was white, but now its soft hairs were shed and its hide was grey. Its mother was an albino; she had pink eyes. She hunted usually with Jarrk the bull-seal, and when not hungry they played together for hours, hunting one another around bases of rocks and chasing each other's tails as they swished in bubbled circles that set long ribbons of weed waving and curling and little green crabs scuttling for shelter.

Now the white seal and her cub followed Jarrk into the tidal drift beyond the reef. It was the first time the cub had swum out to sea, the first time it had seen the flash of a salmon. It kicked its linked-flippers and stroked with its skin-flap arms as fast as it could.

They swam with common seals, blotched yellow-brown smaller creatures among the longer grey seals of the Island. Some had come from the coast of Lyonesse and Hercules Promontory, following runs of salmon which came in from the open sea and turned north, seeking their river estuaries.

A slow flicker, a dull gleam with thin strokes of light active beside it, made Jarrk and his mate and cub swim upwards to see what it was. The bull-seal came to rest on the top of his upward sweep with a backward curve that was most pleasurable; for seals, except when they are grown very old and near to death, take great delight in thrusting themselves through water for the upward quiescent glide. Water is not their true or original element: they are warm-blooded animals which ran about on land, and took to water, and which for hundreds of centuries have been acquiring sea-form. The young seal is frightened of water and perhaps would never swim were it not dragged there, moaning miserably, scruff held in mother's teeth, while father grunts in approval and solicitude as he bounces and flaps along beside his family. The little seal enjoys the water very soon, and the joy remains until the time for its final return to the cave of its birth; and there it grows cold like the boulders and skulls around it.

Jarrk swung up on a happy curve of strength, followed by the white seal and her cub. They were invisible to the great conger eel above them. The conger, whose name was Garbargee, was playing with a spring fish which was turning on its side and then on its back, recovering to swim erratically away, to falter, and sink again. A common seal had chopped the salmon as it darted down a submerged chasm of the reef and turned back from a second seal. The seal had torn away its ventral bite, the salmon had staggered away. The tide swept it from the Race. It tried to face the tide, but the nerves of its left lateral line were paralysed, it was weak from shock and drowning. Garbargee the conger eel—who lived at the mouth of the Two Rivers estuary, his favourite pitch being the weedy chain of the Bar Bell Buoy—tasted the salmon's blood as he gulped water in breathing. Sinuating up the stream of tasty water, the conger came to the dying salmon and pulled a bite from its wound. Garbargee was not hungry, having gorged a small conger, four feet long and as thick as a strong man's arm, two hours before, when he had come upon it beside the corpse of a sea-cow which had drifted two thousand miles on the Gulf Stream since death.

Garbargee was a cannibal eel; he weighed over a hundred pounds. He had outgrown his fear of seals, although he still swam away when he smelled or saw one. There were two greyish scars across his back where once Jarrk, finding him in one of the rusty boilers of a warship sunken off the Island, had tried to chop him. The seal's jaws could not open wide enough, and the canine teeth had made two parallel lines in the eel's tough and slimy skin. Garbargee had bitten one of the flap-hands of the seal, and broken two of the prolonged finger-bones, which had healed, but set irregularly. Ever afterwards when swimming idly, for pleasure, Jarrk did not swim straight, but slightly in a curve, owing to the deformity.

Jarrk recognized Garbargee, and let out a bark. He often barked under water, usually when playing with the white seal or one of his mates or would-be mates. He roared both on top and under water when fighting and chasing another bull-seal, and the barking roar was visible by a gust of bubbles which he blew from his teeth and whiskers.

Garbargee felt the driving strokes of the seal's flippers coming nearer. He abandoned the salmon, and swam downwards. Jarrk reached the listless fish, caught it across the back, bit through its backbone, knew it was dead already, and swam down to the sea's bed to eat the fish. He chewed and swallowed for several minutes, during which time his heart-beats slowed to ten a minute, for his blood was rich in oxygen; after which he rose to the surface to breathe. As he swam down he saw a series of dull gleams in the darkness below, and recognized the conger eel.

Garbargee swam away with the salmon bite still in his mouth. He reached a cleft of rock, and lay there, holding himself still by his pectoral fins. His body was curved for an instant propulsion, should the seal find him. With one eye he watched the forward area of water, with the other eye he stared upward. One eye saw the quicksilvery form of Jarrk's swimming at a downward slant, his bubble-whisker'd head searching from side to side; while the other eye watched the broken fish turning in an eddy of the current, head down.

Jarrk passed over and behind Garbargee, and out of sight. Garbargee lay still, his gills and mouth scarcely opening. A drove of wrasse swam down with the current, glinting as first one fish then another turned on its side to take the smaller fish they were pursuing. A lobster walked over his back, but Garbargee did not move. The waterlogged oar of a ship's boat came bumping and turning sideways over the rocks, grey streams of barnacles hanging along its length. It moved into the area of total reflection, opaque darkness beyond an angle of 22½° from the eel's eye. Then Garbargee saw with his right eye a small shape swim into his window or arc of vision, becoming a little seal which shone in streaks as it turned. Strings of bubbles from its nostrils ran over its head and wobbled upwards into the broken dull shiningness of the sea-surface.

Remembering this shape for a small seal, Garbargee slid forward over the rocks, moving with the tide. Strips of ribbon weed as long as himself, fixed to rock by thongs, were waving aslant the current. He swam through the shell-crusted ribs of a ship which had foundered there two centuries before, a French corsair sunken by the cannon of a British privateer. The wreck was another of the homes of Garbargee. Once, by holding his tail round one of the timbers, he had pulled out straight an eight-inch hook, baited with herring, which he had swallowed. The barb had pierced the maxillary bone of his left jaw. Two fishermen in a boat, pulling on the line, had fallen backwards, to haul in a straightened hook of soft steel a quarter of an inch in diameter, a piece of gristle wedged in its barb.

Garbargee swam slowly through the weedy ribs and, reaching the stem, turned into the tide to follow the little seal above. With open mouth the conger approached the cub, which, seeing him, departed as fast as flippers could drive it. Garbargee gave chase. The little seal plunged and twisted, but Garbargee followed every movement, snapping to grip it across the small of its back as it turned. Garbargee meant to catch the cub and take it down to the wreck, where he would tear out its life. But the white seal, its mother, searching for her cub, crossed the line of chase, and, seeing her, Garbargee swam down and slithered into impregnable holding under the wreck.

The white seal led the cub to the surface, uneasily turning down to swim under it, watchful for attack. Amidst the waves they lay, taking in air: then she leapt upon the cub, rolling over and clasping it between her flippers, nuzzling it and biting its head in joy and anger for the scare given her. The dark head of Jarrk looked up beside them, and they talked together, eyeing the moon and shaking drops from their whiskers, peering about with dim out-of-water sight. The shine of a salmon jumping sharpened three heads towards it. Before the splash was smoothed in the wave the heads had vanished.

Garbargee, lying behind the weed-streaming stem of the wreck, saw the shape of Salar reform in a surge of bubbles, and watched it moving away in sea-paleness to the east, towards the estuary, followed by ten smaller fish, led by Gralaks the grilse.

3 *Coastal Shallows*

Now sometimes a fish fails to find the way to its parent river because it has lost the guiding currents of familiar fresh water, spreading root-like into the sea. When Salar came in from the Atlantic feeding banks the rivers of that coast were low, for little rain had fallen since the New Year. Owing to raids of seals he had left prematurely the meeting place of currents in the Island Race, and now he was travelling in a bay where the fresh-water layers gave no memory-pressures to his brain. He swam on without direction, followed by the school of young salmon which was making for the coast. The grilse were in familiar water, for here as smolts they had travelled during the year before.

Salar, disturbed by a current of colder water in which he had swum, turned across to avoid it. Gralaks, entering the cold current a few lengths behind the big salmon, half rolled and then thruddled up and leapt for joy. The other grilse did likewise. This was water of the Two Rivers, their mother stream, their home!

Salar cruised on slowly, alone. He rose to the surface and flopped out, falling back on his side, irritated by the sea-lice clinging to his skin behind the ventral fins and on the descending taper of his back. Each grilse falling back made a bubbled or seething hole, entering head first, with little splash: this was the joy leap; whereas Salar made the smacking splash of an aimless fish.

He swam on, having crossed the layer of colder, less dense water, and came to warmer salt again. Seeing a pollack above him, he curved up and while on his side gripped it across the back. But he was not hungry; his flesh was stored full of power; it was oozing in curd between his muscles. He expelled the pollack from his mouth, caught it up again head first, and then, after hesitation, closed his gill-covers and the expulsion of water pushed it out. He swam on slowly, a lost salmon.

After four hours he had swum east nearly twenty miles, and

reached the first drifts of broken sea-shells on the sea's bed. The quality of light in the sea was changing, as it had changed in water throughout his life. White opaqueness of moon, with the particular glints and gleams it gave on fish and weed and wave-hollow, was being absorbed in a general greyness of the sea. The fish's window or conning area of visibility was becoming clearer, but part of his life was leaving him with the dimming of the moon. Colour was coming back into the sea with the daylight. He swam on without purpose.

He came into an area of strong coastal currents, and turned with them. They swept over jags of rocks faster than his slow cruising speed. This was the race over Dead Man's Reef. Had Salar chanced to stray here a few hours later or earlier he would have entered the current running north and gone with it along the rocky shore and past the Morte Stone and so to the Severn Sea, where he would have found the fresh-water guides to his parent river. Now a strong race was setting south, and not liking white or broken water, Salar turned into the tide, and swimming with it, he came to sandy shallows ribbed by the periodic sway and roll of waves. His nervous liquid-cells knew the rhythm of these waves; it was the same rhythm of the Severn Sea, the pulse of shallow Atlantic rollers at the full of the moon. He leapt through a wave, a gleaming impulse of joy. Through a shoal of very thin and small greenish fish he sped, amusing himself by sucking in some and expelling them from his mouth: a greeting, for as a smolt he had chased and fed upon the translucent gravel-sprats with their greenish dots of eyes. He drove through a shoal of bass feeding on the sprats, which were trying to escape their spine-backed enemies by darting down at the sand and burying themselves with a rapid wriggle. He scattered the bass, remembering how as a smolt he had been terrified by their large-mouthed hunger in the tideway.

So he came to shallow water where the rollers were rising sheer and top-creaming before assembling themselves for a final assault of the shore. Gulls were flying slowly up and down the white spreads of surf, turning on black wing-tips and peering down with yellow-colourless eyes for living or dead food. Seeing the salmon leaping on the far side of a wave, the carrion feeders uttered cries as colourless and envious as their eyes.

Of birds, the herring gulls are the most selfish, all the harmony of their lives is in their flight. They never play; they search the edge of the sea and the land for themselves alone. They find peace at sunset. On spread wings, gliding, or flying slowly through the evening air in formation, calmly and in silence they return to their roosting ledges in cliffs, above the sea whose entire being is fretful. The gulls have risen from the land to find aerial beauty, while the sea grows more bitter-blind with the centuries.

Salar played through the green walls of the waves. Sea-trout sped through sand-stirring water before him, and flatfish lay still, their backs speckled as sand, invisible. The sea-trout had been born in the rivers, hatched out of eggs in gravel beside salmon eggs. Some were brown trout which by chance had descended to the estuary and assumed a silver coat; others had the salt-itch in them from the egg, offspring of a tribe which had sought sea-food for so long that now it was an instinct. The sea-trout roved in schools, living a merry life round the coast until the time came to return home for spawning. One of the biggest sea-trout of the Two Rivers was Trutta, the great spotted pug, who was to become the friend of Salar and Gralaks, in Denzil's Pool, and then in the water above Humpy Bridge, and later, in the pool called Fireplay.

The sun rose over the hills of the mainland, and splashed its gold on the walls of the waves. Salar swam on, leaping several times in every mile, curving out of the water and curving back. This was the travel leap; he used the weight of falling back to drive him onwards. He must leap: shocks of energy passed through his body, stimulated by the pulses of creation passing through the water: memory-excitations of sand-stirring water, of light-play on corrugations of gravel. He was a smolt again, a sea-sprite.

The sudden appearance of this sea leaper startled a bird that was paddling aimlessly in the foamy back-drag of creaming wave-tops. It hastened seawards, padding a score of times and then ceasing through weariness. The bird had thick waterproof plumage and a long sharp beak; a guillemot. Its head, neck, and back were dark brown; its breast, which should have been white, was also dark brown, in clotted streaks of featherlets. When it had been white-breasted the guillemot had enjoyed movement in air and water; now it was cold, weary unto death, the filaments of its feather were stuck together with oil-fuel waste cast overboard by a ship. The guillemot had swum up from its chase of fish into a floating mass of crude petroleum, and thereafter it flew no more; its skin was painful, winds and tides drifted it away from its parent island, it starved. Three years before it had nearly caught the little smolt Salar as he swam with his brethren in the strange currents of the Race; now Salar, leaping near it, shocked some of its remaining life from it. He swam on under the guillemot, seeing its two feet and air-glistening body mingled with the reflections of feet and body. Later the bird was thrown on the beach by the surge and dragged itself about until the shore-rats found it dying and feasted on it; soon it was water, air, sand, salt again.

Round the rocks a current was sweeping, and this Salar followed. He swam an oar's length from the base of cliffs strewn with submerged rocks on which limpets and other shell fish were creeping. Anemones were open, waving arm-rays to seize little fish and wandering shrimps. A fisherman standing on a flat rock above the sea and pulling up a lobster pot saw him jump out of the water and cursed with envy. Gulls were soaring and crying above the cliffs, for the fishermen had disturbed the nesting ledges whereon they were beginning to imagine their young. Seeing the salmon leap below, some of the cockbirds dropped down and flew to and fro over the water; for when bass showed there, they were feeding on surface shoals of smaller fish, and the gulls fed among them. The salmon resembled bass, although bass did not usually leap from the water.

Michael J. Loates

Salar cruised on, jumping not so often, as his excitement at finding shallow water grew less. Stimulated by the vivid pulse of his blood, his parasites secured their holds between his scales and sucked that blood. He leapt and fell back on his side with a splash that set the gulls screaming in envious competition. A couple of hundred yards farther on he jumped and smacked down on the water again, this time on his other side. To the lice Salar was the earth, a benevolent and inanimate cosmos which yielded nourishment when cultivated and stimulated with chemical injections. Their earth supported them; they knew the pleasures of feeding and sleeping, and the greater joy of perilous love-seeking and satisfaction. For the search for love involved a slow crawl from scale to scale, while their earth was liable to flex into swift movement and the water strike them violently; their bodies were armoured. Salar carried seventeen sea-lice on his body. Most of them were females which had been successfully sought by the smaller males, since each of the females carried twin strings of eggs. Some male lice had lost their grip during the struggle for courtship, and had died of starvation near the Azores.

Salar came to another tide-race off the headland along whose length he had been cruising, and swam south with it. A common seal spied him by the reef called Bag Leap, but he sped away downtide, and feeling the lightness of a fresh-water stream which was moving inshore against the press of the tide, swam with it, keeping near the rocks of the south side of the headland. And cruising against the current he overtook a school of smaller fish which he knew by their shape and flexion. They were leaping and playing, led by Gralaks the grilse, for they were now in their mother-stream, water of the Two Rivers.

Wizzle the Chakcheck, the peregrine falcon, saw the blue-grey shapes moving in the water as he cut his hard swift circles in the sky over the precipice of his eyrie. He saw the rocks under green water as dark blotches. His sight was stereoscopic, keenest of the sun. He could see pigeons flying above the town up the estuary twelve miles away in clear air.

The gift of sight is the sun's greatest gift to the world; it is only by the sense of sight that man clears himself; Truth is clarity, which is beauty.

The sun shone on falcon and fish, greensward and glint of rock; pride of the sun was in them. Chakcheck saw the blue back of his mate shoot out of the cliff below, from the eyrie on Bone Ledge which gravely she had been meditating. It was the time of vernal equinox, light and dark were balanced, the sun's eye was to gaze longer every day: the solar stare was life. Seeing his mate Chakcheck tipped up and fell over sideways in a dive upon her. She dived to get speed, then shot up in the wind pouring up the rock face, to meet him. They approached one another at a leisurely speed of a hundred and fifty miles an hour. They met and paused, the tiercel checked, the falcon fell; and together they dived to the water, flattening out and skimming a wave crest, and using the currents, eddies, rebuffets, and pillars of the wind, rose without pinion-throw a thousand feet and in the blast stayed, cutting darkly into the day.

They saw Kronk the raven watching them from the lookout scaur near his nest, where his mate was sitting on five eggs hugged between her thighs, her blood fevered with hope. They saw a cormorant paddling in the waves, watching them as it rested before tipping up and swimming down in pursuit of fish. They saw the blurred shape of the common seal swimming round the base of a rock; and, beyond the buoy marking the sunken reef of Bag Leap, something which made them, in playful mood, slip off their wind ledge and fall to see what they were—black lengths rolling up, spray-blowing, and rolling under again. This was a herd of porpoises, led by Meerschwein the old herring hog. The peregrines cut circles above the porpoises; the tiercel dived at Meerschwein in scornful play, rose on the gusts of the south-west as though abruptly ending this wind foolery, and turned and swept away north-east at a hundred and ten miles an hour, followed by the falcon. Wizzle wanted a pigeon from the oak-grown valley inland.

The porpoises were following a large school of salmon making for the Two Rivers estuary. More than sixty fish were travelling fast before the black glistening bottle-noses, which drove forward in two tiers, one layer or line diving below the other as it rose to the surface to vent. When hunting the porpoises breathed thrice every sea-mile. The lower tier swam under the salmon, gathering together again after a massed drive. Appearing suddenly from invisibility below, the porpoises scattered the salmon in terror surface-wards, where they were pursued and chopped by the upper tier.

Behind the herd of porpoises, travelling fast, was Orca Gladiator, the grampus, the killer, blowing a jet of spray into the air as it rose to breathe every quarter of a mile.

Salar, swimming easily with the grilse, was startled when a hen-salmon bigger than himself thruddled past him, swung round, and dived to the gravel below, where she remained with her tail round a rock. He sped away forward, followed by the grilse, and then sank to the gravel of a clearing, three fathoms down, in order to see the enemy afar. One eye looked up and forward, the other eye watched midwater and flank. Beside and behind him lay the grilse, resting on gravel touched by their ventral fins, their tails slightly curved, ready for instant acceleration.

When other fish swam into sight Salar knew by the way they dashed about what the enemy was. Meerschwein and the herd of porpoises had harried Salar's shoal when they had been herring-hunting. Aimless fear possessed Salar as it had the grilse. They waited with curved tails. A glistening shape drove forward bubble-shaking: and where the salmon had been resting gravel and shell-speck swirled thickly.

But as he was swimming under a ledge of rock in deeper water Salar came face to face with Orca Gladiator, who had just crushed a porpoise in its great teeth and swallowed the mid part of the body, leaving the head to float away on one side of its jaws, and the tail-flukes on the other. Orca was eighteen feet long and when it could get salmon to eat, it ignored other creatures, except occasionally to chop them in fun. The grampus had followed porpoises for some weeks, having come from the fogs of the Labrador coast, where the icebergs were drifting down from the Arctic Ocean. In those cold waters it had been one of a pack hunting whales, which they tore bit by bit, launching themselves at the leviathan of warm flesh, biting and tugging and worrying until each jawful was free.

Instantly Salar turned and shot away, but Orca was as quick, lunging forward under the salmon. Salar leapt thrice from the wide peg-toothed gape, each time nearly falling back into the jaws. He flickered and doubled, and scurried under an over-hanging rock, and lay there with fast-beating heart, hidden by a fringe of bladder weed swaying gently in the tide. His head and body were in half darkness, and pressed against the rock worn concave by the scour of sand and water at low tide. Orca tried to get him, but the head of the grampus was big, round, and blunt: vainly it wallowed about the rock, shoving and blowing the sand. It rose through the waves and gave a loud snorting grunt and swam out to sea, at a tangent to the direction taken by the porpoises. About a mile from the rocks it turned and swam back slowly, swinging down to the base of the ledge where the body and tail of Salar were still moulded in fear against the rock. It came to the surface, grunting angrily, and swam once more, to swim up and jump clear of the water, showing its black fluked tail and mackerel-like shape in a wide splash. It swam away fast, throwing itself over lines of waves it crossed diagonally in pursuit of the porpoises.

Half an hour later a fisherman in a small boat off the North Tail of the estuary of the Two Rivers watched seven 'erring 'ogs playing with a large clean-run springer not a hundred yards from where he was fishing. The 'erring 'ogs, he told his companions later in the inn, lay roughly in a ring. First one would take the living fish in its mouth and throw it up: a second would catch it, toss it in the air, the others would roll up and bump it with their snouts. Once the fish got away, but was caught again under water, and the game continued nearer his boat. After a while the 'ogs tore a bite out of the fish. Then a master great 'og, four or five times as big as the others and big round as a tar-barrel, came up and they cleared like as if the devil was after them. When they had gone the fisherman tried to pick up the salmon, which was floating head down, on its back, white belly showing, but there was too much swell and broken water on the Tail. As the tide was beginning to flow strong, he hoisted sail and went home to the fishing village with the news of what he had seen. Other fishermen had seen the porpoises, too, and there was much swearing. The lawful season for nets was not yet begun, and here was the spring run of fish, no water in the rivers for them to go up, being protected by law for the sake of they bliddy 'errin' 'ogs.

Fishermen had been taking salmon in the estuary in nets at that time of year for scores of centuries before the Two Rivers Conservancy Board had made its by-laws.

4 Estuary Night

An hour before midnight, in bright moonlight, a dozen crews of four men each, silently in rubber thighboots, went down to their salmon boats moored on the sandbank at the edge of the deep water of the fairway. "Let'n come," said one, truculently, with a glance up the estuary. All the fishermen felt an angry but subdued sense of injustice against water-bailiffs employed by the Board of Conservators. They believed that the laws were imposed only for the benefit of rich sportsmen; while they themselves were poor men with families to feed and clothe from what they got by fishing. The Board, they said, stops us fishing before the big fall run of fish, declaring they must run through to spawn; but the rod-and-line men aren't stopped for six weeks after the nets be off. Yet when the spring run begins, they stop us fishin' for to stock the rivers for the rich gentry's pleasure. So most of the fishermen ignored the limits of the season for net-fishing, and fished for salmon all the year through when the weather was favourable. During the close season they fished only at night, beginning two hours before low ebb, and continuing until the returning flow made the drag on the nets too heavy. The tide ebbed brightly; the water looked white, the shapes of boats going down were indiscernible. There was no wind. The night was in the moon's unreal power. Curlew and other wading birds were crying on sandbank and gravel ridge. In each boat two men pulled at the sweeps, a youth sat in the bows, the owner sat in the stern, where the net was piled.

An old man in the stern of one boat sat upright as light flicked on the starboard bow and was scattered in a loud splash. The oarsmen, dipping enough to keep way on the boat, looked over their left shoulders. Salar had leapt near the Pool buoy, at the tail of The String, where the ebbing waters of the Two Rivers met and bickered.

Salar had gone up with the estuary tide in daylight as far as

Sunken Tree bend, where the salt water pressing against river water was so cold that he and the grilse had dropped back with the tide, avoiding fresh water and the plates of ice riding down with the river. The salmon's excitement arising from crammed power was chilled by the sleet water. Now in the Pool, below The String, with its irregular line of froth, many salmon were hovering head to stream, avoiding, sometimes playfully, the currents of cold water by rising or swimming sideways or drifting backwards before them, always nosing into the water-flow.

The Sharshook Ridge, a gravel bank bound with mussels, grew longer and higher as the tide ebbed at five knots. The Pool buoy rolled with the weight of assaulting water, leaning ocean-wards on its iron chain which the salt never ceased to gnaw in darkness, sunlight, and the moon's opalescent glimmer. Ocean's blind purpose is to make all things sea; it understands nothing of the Spirit that moves in air and water.

On the shillets of the lower ridge known among fishermen as the Fat and the Lean, the keel-shoe of the salmon boat grated, the man in the bows sprang out and held the gunwale. The boat swung round to the shore, noisy with the water streaming against its length. When the other three men had clambered out, he shortened the anchor rope in the ring and carried the anchor a little way up the slope of the ridge, putting it down carefully lest the clank of metal be heard over the water. The tide was too strong for shooting a draught, and they waited there quietly, talking in low voices and sometimes standing silent to listen for sound of the water-bailiff's motor-boat.

Soon the boat was heeling over, and they shoved it down into the lapsing water. Splash! My Gor, that was a master fish, thirty pound by the noise of'n. Shall us shoot, feyther? Bide a bit, 'tes rinning too strong yet.

They waited. The youth struck a match to light a cigarette. Put'n out, I tell 'ee! Aw, I ban't afraid of no bliddy bailies. Nor be us, but us wants fish to-night, don't us? 'Tes no sense hadvertisin' us be yurr, be ut? Okay. American films were shown nightly in the converted shed called The Gaiety Theatre. The youth wished he had a machine-gun in the bows of the boat for the water-bailiffs.

Other boats were going down, gliding fast on the ebb and in silence but for the occasional squeak of sweeps in thole pins. A flight of shelduck went by overhead, wind sibilating in a wing where a quill had dropped. Far away down the estuary the piping and trilling of birds running and feeding by the wavelap line was changing to cries of

41

alarm as the first boats reached their stances on shore and sandbank. Two sets of flashes beyond the hollow roar of the bar came from lighthouses north and south of the Island twenty miles away. There was no horizon to the earth, no shape or form to its objects, the moon's light was dead light.

Fish were dropping back with the tide, new schools were coming in over the bar, on whose pitted and shifting sandbanks the lines of waves plunged and broke with a roar, filling the shimmering hollow midnight.

In lessening tide the boat put out, leaving one man on the ridge. He took a turn of the rope round back and shoulder, trod a firm stand, and gripped the rope in his hands, watching the boat drifting down and across and shedding net from stern as it glided into luminous obscurity. It was a flake of darkest shadow in the moon-dazzle on the water, and then was lost to sight. He braced himself and affirmed his footholds, to take the weight of water on rope and net which hung

aslant in the tide, between head-rope buoyed with corks and heel-rope weighted with lead. The boat turned into the tide, and he leaned against the curved drag of the net with its two-inch mesh stipulated by Conservancy by-law for the escape of smolts.

He heard the noise of the boat touching uptide, the others clambering out, the clank of anchor, and one of his mates hastening to help him. Together they took strain on the rope and waited for their mates, who were trudging down to meet them with the other rope. The arc cast by the two hundred yards of net was now an elongated and narrowing bulge, which must be drawn in as quickly as possible before any fish enclosed by the netting walls found a way out by the space between ropes and the ends of the net.

They hauled slowly, steadily, hand under hand, leaning back against the scarcely yielding ropes, pulling against an area of water restrained by eight hundred thousand meshes. The two coconut fibre ropes came in four yards a minute. Each rope ended at a wooden stretcher, to which were tied the head-rope and the heel-rope. At every concerted tug on these less water was restrained, and the net came in not so dead. Now the skipper became more anxious, and ordered two of the crew to haul at the heel-rope to foreshorten the net under any fish which might be dashing about the enclosed water. The men at the heel-rope hauled rapidly, bending down, their hands near the gravel to keep the bottom of the net as low as possible. The seine, or purse net, came in swiftly, seeming to hiss in the water. There was nothing in the net.

The fishermen showed no disappointment. They had been wet in sea-labour since boyhood. The youth fetched the boat and they shook small crabs and seaweed from the net and repiled it in the stern of the boat. After a few minutes' rest they shot another draught, and hauled in again, bending low as before when the seine came fast and easy near the top of the water, which was asplash and glinting: they lifted the seine and ran back a few paces, while the youth dropped on hands and knees, and gripping a fish by the wrist, his thumb by the tail-fin, lugged it out and struck vigorously the base of its head with a wooden thole pin. It ceased to slap the gravel, and lay still. He killed four other fish, three of them being grilse. A good draught! One twenty-pounder, another fifteen, and the others between five and six pound apiece.

The fish were flung in the well of the boat, and covered with sacks.

Two more draughts were shot, taking three more fish, one of

them a lean brown kelt with fungus growing on tail-fin and jaw. They knocked the kelt on the head, and threw it into the water. The kelt had entered fresh water as a clean-run fish weighing eighteen pounds a year previously; it languished in the lower pools of the river all spring and summer, and travelled at the fall to the spawning redds under the moor. During the twelve months it had lived on its stored power; when taken in the net it weighed under ten pounds. A few of the older fishermen killed kelts because it was a Conservancy law that kelts, or unclean fish, must be returned to the sea. One or two very old fishermen remained in the village who refused to believe that a kelt could mend itself in salt water, and return again the following season as a clean fish. They said it was another lie of the Board to take away the living of poor men. The hard times in which these old fellows had been schooled were passed away, but their effect would remain throughout the rest of their lives.

After a pause of slackwater, the tide began to flow, and with the flow came Salar and the school of grilse led by Gralaks, forerunners of larger schools to arrive from the feeding banks in later spring.

Salar and the eight grilse swam a little ahead of the flow, to breathe and control the current. Suddenly alarmed by a fearful apparition, Salar shot up and across, breaking the water with a bulging splash and a glittering ream or travelling wavelet. Gralaks also leapt, and the watchers saw the arrowy glints of their reaming. They saw too a broader, slower flash, and thought this to be the roll of an immense fish. The boat was already afloat, the rowers waiting at the sweeps, the fourth man holding the post-staff. Immediately the boat put out, the rowers bending the sweeps with full strength across the tide, then with it, and back across: they shipped sweeps and ran ashore: the skipper threw out the anchor and hastened to help the fourth man. They heard and saw splashing, and imagined a great haul, bigger than the record of seventeen fish a few years before. As they hauled he exhorted the heel-rope men in a voice hoarsely earnest to pull faster, and together. Although only half the net was in, they could feel the jags on the walls as fish struck them trying to escape.

Then a shout from the direction of the Pool told them of danger: the water-bailiffs had landed on the ridge. The fishermen did not fear being fined if caught and convicted: they dreaded confiscation and destruction of their net, and their licence for the season, soon to open, not being renewed.

Glancing over his left shoulder, the skipper saw several moving spots of light from electric torches, and realized the bailies were there in force. He knew they could not search without a warrant, and he could plead he was rough-fish-catching; but if the bailies arrived while they were giving salmon a dapp on the head, they would have all the proof, needed. Gladly he heard the sound of raised voices upalong, and hoarsely exhorted the others to get the seine in, and away. He began to speak rapidly to himself, wife and children needing food and covering, one law for the rich another for the poor, but if they bailies comed near they'd find what they wasn't looking for. An extra-ordinary plunging and beating of the water inside the distorted horseshoe of corks made him pause in his mental tirade, and haul the stronger on his rope. He realized something other than fish was in the seine; the tugging plunges against the net made him anxious lest it be broken.

The shouts from the upper end of the ridge had ceased; the water-bailiffs, having come upon a boat with net piled for a draught, were moving down, hoping to find one in the act of taking salmon.

'Errin' 'ogs, cried the skipper, with a roar of disgust. Fetch the boat, he ordered his son. Seven porpoises were clashing and threshing about in the seine. Gralaks was there, too, her sides and shoulders scored criss-cross where she had driven against the net and broken her scales. Quick, into the boat, cried the skipper, shouting as a spot of approaching light wavered and dazzled his eyes an instant. Holding the head-rope, he shoved off and scrambled aboard. Pull like something, he cried, taking a turn with the head-rope round a thwart, and hauling over the stern. The skipper did not swear—he was Chapel through and through, as he occasionally informed those who did. Several torchlights were flashing as the water-bailiffs hastened over the gravel bank, wary of falling into pits left by the barges digging gravel. Make'n spark, cried the skipper, and the rowers grunted with their efforts. Then, seeing that the net was safe, the skipper bellowed indignantly, Why don't you chaps stop they witherin' 'errin' 'ogs, can you answer me that, tho'?

The youth wanted to leave the net trailing in the water, to taunt the bailies into giving chase, and then clog the screw of their motor-boat with the mesh. Tidden no sense, grunted his father, who was in shape not dissimilar from the shape of a herring hog. Besides, the tide be flowin', if 'twere ebbin', might be some use, 'twould serve the bailies right to be drov' out to sea and wrecked.

The net was taken aboard, with one small porpoise, which was soon battered to death, and the boat made for the sandbank below the sea-wall of the village.

There they were met by the skipper's wife, who whispered in a voice deep and hoarse that two bailies with a policeman were waiting by the slip, up which they must walk to get home. They witherin' bailies, they deserve to get their boat rammed and zunk below 'em, declared the skipper in great disgust.

The salmon were taken from under the sack. While the two hands and the youth lit cigarettes at a discreet distance, the skipper's wife removed a wide black skirt much speckled with dried fish-scales. Rapidly the skipper threaded a stout cord through gill and mouth of each salmon. The cord was then tied round the wife's waist, after which the skirt, by a feat of balancing made more difficult on the wet and infirm sand, was put on and fastened. Having anchor'd the boat, and carrying the oars, the crew went slowly towards the slip leading to the quay.

"What have you got in that bag?" one of the waiting water-bailiffs demanded, pointing to the bulging sack on the skipper's shoulder.

"My own property," replied the skipper.

"Of what nature?"

"'Og."

"I don't want no sauce," threatened the bailiff. "I have a constable here. What's in that sack?"

"'Og, I tell 'ee."

"Turn it out."

"You can't make me. Where's your search warrant?"

"I know what you've got. You're caught this time. Do you want me to go to a magistrate and get a warrant, when you'll lose your renewal of licence. I'll ask you once more, what have you got in that sack?"

"'Og, I tells 'ee. For a bailie's breakfast, if you likes."

"Turn it out."

"If you promises to fry it for to-morrow's breakfast."

"I promise nothing."

"Why don't you try and search me?" screeched the old woman, amidst laughter.

"For the last time I ask you, will you turn out that bag?" shouted the water-bailiff. "Or shall I give you in charge?"

"Aw, don't 'ee vex yourself so," said the skipper, in a gentle voice. "Here's an Easter egg for 'ee," and he dropped the heavy weight, and tugged the sack from the blubbery mass.

"It's yours, Nosey Parker," yelled the fishwife, as she staggered away, holding the arm of her husband and laughing stridently.

The curlews made their spring-trilling cries over the water flowing fast up the estuary. Soon the birds would be flying to the high moor for nesting.

Salar swam up with the tide, alone. Within and around and making the muscle-cluster of his body were fats and albuminous matter sufficient for five hundred and seventy ascents of the river, without restoration by feeding, from its mouth in the sea to its source on the moor. The moon declined to the west, and the estuary was silent.

5 *Lamprey*

Again Salar went up to the tide-head, again he shifted back with the ebb to avoid cold streams of fresh water. Ice held earth and water while the moon wore away to a dark shell of itself. Salmon waited for warmer water, birds for warmer air, flowers for warmer earth. Spring was held down by frost.

Salar knew now the meaning of a net, and he avoided those places in the estuary where a strange enemy dropped slowly down the water, behind a more fearsome enemy, in shape between bird and seal, which moved with a dip of wings or flippers along the surface. Whenever he saw a boat he sped away down the current, seeking a depth of pit or hole from which he watched while resting on the bottom.

As the moon's light grew less, so the tides moved more slowly up the estuary, and with a diminishing press of water. More salmon came over the bar on every flowing tide, with big spotted sea-trout which fed on smaller sea-trout and other fish as they roved the channels between sandbanks and the worm-cast mud of ruined saltings.

Salar became way-wise in the estuary. He returned no more with the ebb to the sandy shallows by the bar, but remained with other fish in the agitation and noise of the two tides meeting above the Pool—for the estuary of one river lay north, the other lay south, and their returning ebbs were in opposition, causing that irregular movement of froth where the tides clashed and jittered, called The String.

At half-tide Salar idled under The String, swung about in eddies and swirls, rising and dipping on trends of the shifting and myriad-varying tide-force. There also schools of bass waited, watching for gravel-sprats, and small fish tumbled down in the twisting and uncertain currents. Other salmon, some marked by nets, waited on the bed of the Pool, cached in neutral water-pockets before juts of rock or boulders. They were uneasy, unspirited, watchful for danger.

A boat sailed slowly up The String, in it a fisherman holding tiller tucked between elbow and side. He held a line in his hand. In his other hand he held a rope, attached to a sail shaking in the wind abeam. On the submerged line was a lead weight, below it a length of catgut, and at the end of the gut was a hook half concealed by an artificial worm of red rubber. A nickel spinner just above the shank of the hook made a bright blur in the water, behind which the worm wriggled. The line slanted in the tide.

Salar did not see the boat until it was nearly over him, then he sped up against the current, turned and went down to the bed of the Pool, to lie behind other salmon whose heads, fins, and flanks had been hurt in escape from nets.

He saw the boat, which was tarred below the water-line, changing in shape and colour as it moved slowly forward. From a scattered blur it assembled into a sharp nose which drew after it splashes and flashes of light amidst its broken surface image. When it was directly overhead it was dark and defined in a skin of slipping light, dreaded porpoise shape. Salar saw the line slanting in the water, light running thinly up and down its length. When the boat had passed out of his inverted cone of vision, he watched the line and saw the artificial bait as something which made him alert and wary.

The fisherman was spinning for bass, which with every flow came over the bar in schools, feeding eagerly on rag-worms, gravel-sprats, shrimps, and small fish. Returning on the ebb, the spiny fish ranged themselves in The String and waited there energetically for food to wriggle into their big mouths.

While Salar was watching the lure, something was watching Salar. This was an enemy he had never seen in his life before—Petromyzon the Stone-sucker. The Greeks were kind when they gave its family that name. Petromyzon was a relative of the Hag-fishes, creatures with a low organization of skeleton. Petromyzon was like an eel, or a worm, a huge torpid worm. Its body resembled the artificial rubber thing escaped from the fisherman's hook, magnified, dis-coloured, sunk in living slovenliness, animated waste-product of the spirit of life. Petromyzon had a scaleless body and a sucker mouth thorny with teeth for rasping off scales and flesh and drawing the blood of fishes. It had no jaws or ribs. It had no real bone in its body. It drew breathing-life through seven-a-side bronchial openings instead of gills. It had a single nostril at the top of its head. Now, stuck to a stone on which grew bladder weed hiding its head, Petromyzon was waiting to sneak up on Salar and clamp itself to the richness of his body.

It clung to the stone, moving its tongue backwards and forwards for suction. Salar lay behind another stone half an oar's length in front of Petromyzon. The bed of the Pool under the meeting tides was quiet at three-quarter ebb. Above Salar loose weed and small fish, after being swung and swirled in the tidal bicker, were moving fast in the confluent westerly currents; but in the hollow of the Pool's bed there was an area of quiet. On stones and sodden carbonizing trunks and roots of trees, washed out of river-banks in old floods, and now half-buried in gravel, the seaweed lifted in lightly rising water; the salmon resting there were on the point of lifting, their air-bladders repressed to resist the upward trend. On the eastern edge of the Pool, however, the water of the backwash was moving in an opposite direction to the tide; and here fish were facing down the estuary. In one place, by the rusty stock of an old iron-and-wood anchor, Gralaks the grilse was hovering between two layers of water moving at different rates, and facing north; while a large spotted sea-trout less than a fathom below the grilse was facing south. These fish were using the vagaries of the currents to maintain them with the least effort.

Salar lay where the moving fronds of weed stroked the azure-white skin of his belly. Within his body, and under the fore-part of his backbone, was a cavity or air-bladder which automatically adjusted itself to the lift of the water: thus he was able to continue floating a few inches above the stone, for the pleasing sensation of being touched by the seaweed.

Every moment the pockets and eddies of the tide were changing with the altering set of currents. Automatically the salmon shifted with them. The two fish by the old anchor moved away as a gravel ridgelet which had been piling up beside the anchor was suddenly scoured by a flume of water that straightened out the eddy; small stones, sand, and broken shells whirled away. A ruinous wickerwork crab-pot was uncovered, the ridgelet's foundation. As the water cut away the gravel, so the wickerwork leaned and loosened, to lurch away over the stones and come slowly to rest on the bed of the Pool between Salar and Petromyzon.

Petromyzon loosened its ringed mouth on the stone, and slithered towards the broken crab-pot, while Salar continued to buoy himself over the waving fronds of seaweed.

A flexible submarine, marbled mud, moved through a hole in

the crab-pot, fourteen streams of water moving in and out of its gill-clefts. The thick soft lips of the sucker mouth began to work over the thorn-like teeth. The expressionless eyes were fixed on the salmon's flank. Slowly it moved through the crab-pot. Having no swimming bladder, it could only rise in water by muscular exertion; it quivered, seeming to shorten and thicken, and launched itself at Salar, rearing its head to strike at the scaled side; and instantly clamped itself there.

Salar's acceleration up the Pool, his turn and zigzagging dash down the tide made other salmon leave their resting places and sink together to the bottom, whence they could observe the widest area of water above them. In fear Salar leapt out of the water, causing the boatman holding the line with the red rubber bait to sit upright and puff rapidly at his cold pipe. 'Twas the largest Zeven-Ole I ivver zeed tackle a zalmon, he told them later in the "Royal George".

Salar could not shake off Petromyzon. The lamprey's mouth was stuck firmly to his left side below the medial line of nerves, forward of the ventral fins. Indifferent to the salmon's slipping and turning rushes, to his rolling staggers as he changed from one tide-pressure to another, Petromyzon sucked the scales closer to his teeth, and began to rasp away and swallow skin and curd and flesh. He drew blood, and fed contentedly.

Salar rested on the bed of the Pool, gulping water irregularly, for his fast-beating heart. In front of him the iron links of the Pool buoy chain turned and returned slowly as the buoy above wallowed twisting in the combined weights of two tides. He could see the movements of the hind part of his enemy's body as Petromyzon allowed itself to be borne in moving water, holding securely with its mouth. Starting forward with pain, Salar rolled and tried to scrape off the lamprey against a stone. Although the salmon weighed twenty pounds, his weight in water varied with his speed of movement: he weighed nothing when motionless: so Petromyzon continued to feed with only slight disturbance. Suddenly frenzied by the feeling of lost freedom, Salar swam up to the surface and leapt with all his strength, deliberately to fall back on his side and knock away his enemy. Petromyzon, accustomed since earliest life to irregular motion when attached to its hosts, most of which were quitted only when they died, endured the buffeting and sucked the harder.

After slackwater, and the returning flow, Salar became accustomed to the lamprey. The pain had gone, and he had no more fear of it. Petromyzon was a hindrance, something to be gotten rid of by leaping and by scraping against stones. He was used to the extra drag, to the queerness of moving aslant when he meant to swim straight. In the tide's swilling murkiness he drifted, past lessening sandbanks and muddy glidders, a large quiet fish, as though unseeing among smaller coarse fish feeding eagerly. He moved slowly through the water, scarcely overtaking clusters of seaweed loose in the tide. Under the harmless looming length flatfish flapped along the bottom, feeding squint-eyed amidst racing gravel and sand and the twirling of black oak-leaves.

Off the shingle tongue of Crow, the channel deepened and the tide raced narrow. Salar swam on slowly through the tide, hardly moving. The dark hull of an anchor'd barge loomed noisily before him. He was accustomed now to the shape of large boats. The barge had been taking gravel aboard during low tide, and the crew were awaiting deeper water before sailing up the fairway to the quays of the port. The exhaust of the ship's kerosene engine thudded hollowly, issuing black smoke. Salar felt the thuds in the water as the hull appeared to race over him.

Other salmon were moving up with the tide. Among them was Gralaks the grilse. The large sea-trout which had been hovering behind the wood-and-iron anchor was swimming below her. This was Trutta. He had spawned seven times in his native stream; during seven springs and summers he had escaped death by net, gaff, hook, wire, poison, bomb, otter, seal, porpoise, heron, lamprey, and disease. On each of Trutta's scales was his life-history engraved. His scales, like those of salmon and most other fish, were irregularly circular, resembling the cut section of a tree's trunk. Just as a tree's life or growth can be read by the rings, so does the scale of a fish tell its age. A scale of an old sea-trout, or pug as fishermen of the Two Rivers called it, seen under a microscope showed the growth of its first two years of river-life in the smaller inner rings, with two slight corrosions for the two winters, when food was scarce and its growth was delayed. Thereafter its spawning revisits were indicated by wider corroded rings.

The young sea-trout smolt went down to the sea as the Pleiades were rising in the night sky, and when it returned at full summer, three months later, it had doubled its size. It was then called a peal. The widening rings on its scales showed this sudden increase. During its stay in fresh water the little peal fed on flies and other food, except when it was spawning, but it did not grow any bigger, and when it dropped down to the estuary again in February, the outer edge of its scales were corroded. Sea-feeding soon made it plump, the scales grew to cover that plumpness, and in the following summer it returned once more to its parent stream, there to disport itself with other peal, and amuse itself by taking flies and small fish while waiting for the joys of spawning.

After seven returns to his river Trutta the sea-trout was old and cunning, a thick-headed pug, spotted heavily on gill-cover and flank. His tail-fin was convex, the outer edges worn away. He weighed fourteen pounds. On each scale were seven corrosions, spawning marks, among the wavy rings of easy sea-growth. He was a cannibal, like all his family.

The gleaming grace of Gralaks had first attracted Trutta by the anchor, since when he had followed her. Trutta was scarred thrice by the teeth of lampreys. When in the mudbanks of the middle estuary he saw the tails of small river lampreys waving in the current as they bored in search of rag-worms, he tore them out and champed them and swallowed them. He had a jaw like a pike's jaw and three staggered rows of teeth in the vomer ridge or palate of his mouth. Between these teeth and the curved teeth on his tongue he could grind the flesh from the bones of a peal weighing two pounds without working his jaws.

Higher up the estuary swam Salar, quiet among a drove of bass turning on their sides amidst seaweed, crabs, flatfish, and bubbles streaming from mud-holes of cockles and rag-worms. The tide took him past the wreckage of an abandoned salmon-trap, broken weed-grown hurdles silted in sand around a lagoon, where salmon sometimes rested awhile when returning on the ebb. Old Nog was perched on a black oak post, peering low for fish. Three swans were paddling in the back-wash by the shore, moving down the estuary, while a flock of shelduck bobbed rapidly past on the ribbon-froth of the central current.

The tide poured into a deep pool with a rocky bottom and here the current divided, to flow up a creek which was the mouth of a small river. There was no sand or mud on the bottom because every ebb-tide returning down the Pill swirled against the main fairway ebb, stirring the silt deposited on the river-bed by the previous tide's flow. Mussels grew in clusters on the rock of the pool's bed.

A small boat was riding at anchor in the pool. In it was the fisherman who had seen Meerschwein and the other porpoises play with a salmon off the North Tail a fortnight previously. The fisherman had come to visit his lines put down a few hours before. As Salar approached the boat the fisherman was pulling in one line, with its two score of hooks. Flatfish, pollack, and bass were hooked. One of the bass was but a loose bag of skin and bones attached to a head.

This was the work of Myxine, the glutinous hag of the Two Rivers. The hag was a relation of Petromyzin, but one which lampreys avoided. Myxine's eyes were sunk beneath her skin, deep in the muscles of her head. They were without lenses. Myxine did not need sight, for much of the hag's life was spent within the bodies of fishes. While the bass had been struggling on a hook of the night-line, Myxine had fastened to it and bored a way inside, eating steadily hour after hour until, gorged, she lay at rest in a bag of bones and water. The water poured out as the fisherman lifted it up, and the hag's head, with whisker-like barbels, looked out of the bass's mouth.

The fisherman had never seen such a horrid sight before. With a religious exclamation he dropped it in the boat, and Myxine slithered out of the hollow corpse. He picked the hag up to knock it on the gunwale, but was horrified to find that it was turning itself into a length of slime in his hand.

"Ah, git out, you bissley bigger (beastly beggar), you," muttered the fisherman, shaking the long hair grown to hide his ear-stumps—which had been frozen off during a blizzard aboard a whaler in his youth—as he flung the glutinous hag into the sea.

Myxine swam down to the bed of the pool, and rested there. The act of exuding slime from the thread-cells along her body was additionally exhausting, and the hag lay still, unseen by Salar as he moved slowly in the wedge of tranquil water at the division of currents. Petromyzon waved indolently at his side. Salar had no desire to go up with the tide. His bounding sea-vitality had shrunk within him through fear and the draining wound in his flank. He lay inert on a rock. Half his length away lay Myxine.

The hag saw the waving tail of Petromyzon, and the sight made her teeth work. She got under the lamprey's tail, and fastened her sucker there. Petromyzon lashed, but the hag stuck. In fear Salar started forward. By the time he had reached the sunken lime-kiln by the bend of the sea-wall, half a mile away, Myxine's head was inside Petromyzon's belly.

Salar waited in an eddy beside the rounded broken wall of the kiln, until the rising tide swept through the eddy, and he went on, feeling strangely light.

By the Long Bridge of the port three miles distant he leapt, and a boy on the quay saw what looked like a red poppy on the silver flank. Less than three months later, all of Petromyzon was mud again.

Michael J. Loates

6 *Salvation*

In the night the wind went round from the north to the west and in the morning ice on the saltings and tide-fringes had lost its clarity. Larks sang over the marsh where sheep and ponies no longer grazed tails to wind. A wild bumblebee went humming happily over the wet salt grass. The curlews, whose bubble-link and trilling cries at night arose and fell with the tides, flew away over the hills to the moor, where their cries became more tender. Fishermen in the estuary village hung their nets out on walls and lines between crazy posts of old ships' timbers, looking over the meshes and talking of the seals which were in the estuary.

For Jarrk had come over the bar, as he did every year when the legal net-fishing season was about to open. As the day approached, so the attitude of those men who had been illegally fishing began to change. Why didn't the Board of Conservators see to it that they seals was shot, an old fisherman grumbled. Weren't they poor men trying to earn a living by catching salmon which were scarce enough already, without allowing they bliddy seals and errinogs to come in and drive the fish out to open sea again? Didn't each net owner have to pay five pound a year licence money, to pay the bailies' wages, and what did the bailies do for to earn those wages? Nought but try to stop poor men from getting a few greenbanks in the winter, so that their kids shouldn't rin about the streets barefoot and hungry. If the bailies went out after errinogs and seals they'd save more fish than were took out of season by half a dozen nets. But the Board was there to look after the interests of the rich man's pleasure of whipping water upalong with rod and line, being allowed to fish a month before the net season opened, and six weeks after it had closed; one law for the rich and another law for the poor, aiy, that's it. The younger fisherman did not grumble; they knew more than the old chaps; they stood against walls, relaxing happily in the spring sunshine.

One or two very old fishermen, wearers of ancient cracked leather sea-boots, did not believe that salmon spawned in fresh water, saying it was a yarn put about by the Board to get fish up for the rod and line men. Over their pints they argued that years agone there were lots of fish, but the numbers began to fall off as soon as the barges began digging away the gravel of the Sharshook. That proved, they declared, that salmon laid their eggs under the Sharshook. The grandfathers would not hear any argument about it: the "poor man's right of fishing in the fall, when the big run began, had been stole away by the rich man".

The Board had been formed, and given power to make its own by-laws for the preservation of salmon, when these old fishermen had been boys. Then no water-bailiff had dared venture in the village, nor near the Sharshook at night. Even recently there had been trouble: nine years before, when Trutta the sea-trout was born, the water-bailiffs' boat had been rammed in the Pool one dark night, an attempt to drown them.

Soft spring had come, but still the rivers were low, no water for the fish to ascend. Salar had found the school of grilse again, and with Gralaks and Trutta and other fish went up and down on every tide. The rivers were low and clear, cold with ice and sleet water, the sea was warmer. But every day the river water was growing less cold. Then the seal came in again.

Up the estuary blew the west wind, soft and gracious after the weeks of those winds veering from the north star and twilit polar regions: the hard dryness of north-east, the aerial ice of the north, the brutal shaking gales out of the north-west with its slate-quarry clouds quelling all spirit save in falcons cutting with sharp wings into the blasts. Now the west wind rolled waves in the fairway without tearing their tops; the west wind was a light wind, lifting from air and earth and water the heaviness of winter. The life of the elements was relieved.

Salar leapt through the waves in the bay with hundreds of other salmon playing in release. Few fish were in the estuary. Having scattered the schools, Jarrk returned to the Island Race, where every tide streamed with new silver.

The seal came back behind a school of forty-seven fish which had missed their way home to a Scottish river owing to an irregular set of the Gulf Stream in the Atlantic Ocean. These fish were small-headed, thick-shouldered, their flesh was redder than fish of the Two

Rivers; on the way back they had fed on prawns inhabiting a rock shelf off the Scillies. By chance their forebears had discovered prawns in this place before the glacial caps dissolved on the mountain slopes above their native river; and to the island shelf their ancestral spirit led them on every home-coming.

Exploring the fresh currents in the bay, the agile fish of Tay came into the estuary of the Two Rivers. Jarrk chased one into a lagoon by the South Tail, and ate it lying on a sandbank while the first waves of the flowing tide scoured the sand from under him. The seal was seen by the crew of a boat, and shouted at, but he went on eating, head, shoulders, tail of the fish held in flippers. He ate the eleven-pounder and then launched himself with a flapping jump into the tide-race cutting away the sandbank.

It was the first day of April, and in the estuary and higher salt-water reaches of the Two Rivers the licensed nets were about to shoot their first official draughts of the year. From now until the end of August, the passage of salmon and sea-trout to their rivers would be barred in narrow fairway and streaming shallow by thirty-six nets each eighty fathoms long. Two hours before low tide, during slackwater, and two hours of the new tide, by day and by night, with a close-time from noon Saturday until noon Monday, one or another of thirty-six nets was liable to encircle them.

Jarrk the seal had fished in the estuary of the Two Rivers for more than a dozen years. His serious fishing began with the net season. He knew the voices of many of the fishermen. They had shouted at him often. One boat carried a rifle, and Jarrk knew that boat, recognizing the figure which ran to the boat before he heard the crack and water-thud of the bullet sometimes rising away into the air over his head and piping like a strange bird.

The rifle had been presented to the Board by a sympathizing sportsman and given to the skipper of a crew who claimed to be a skilled marksman. After three years of proximity with salt water, the rifling of its barrel, when examined casually, resembled a railway tunnel blasted through igneous rock. Having fired more than a hundred bullets at the seal, the marksman was wont to remark that the animal dived at the flash. Actually Jarrk, having been scared by the first few water-thuds and occasional ricochets, had ceased to dive from something which was harmless to him.

The seal used to wait until a draught was shot and then swim under the heel-rope weighted with leads and cruise along the bend of netting until he saw a fish. He would remain on the bottom until the arc was short, and the fish dashed about in a small space: then he would swim up and seize it, usually as it tried to turn back between the net and himself. "He picks up fish like a Christian," and "He'll take salmon for a pastime," and "He's a masterpiece for taking fish," the fishermen said. Having caught his fish, the seal lifted up the net and swam away, rising about a hundred yards from the shore and eating it as he lay in the water.

Jarrk went from net to net for his sport. He never entered a net until both post-staffs were drawn ashore. At first he had entered as soon as the fishermen were ashore, and then the fish, dashing in terror along the dark brown web, had escaped inshore where only the rope was striking the surface of the water. So Jarrk, intelligent and percipient—with subtlety of mind developed and widened in every generation since his ancestors, land beasts, had taken to water where were few natural enemies—quickly learned to wait until a net was closed before swimming under it.

The seal came into the estuary for other things besides the sport of hunting salmon. Sometimes at night he lay on the shingle tongue of Crow, listening to the sounds of singing, and concertina music, which came, distinct and clear, over the Pool when the tide was in and no wind blowing. Once he was observed swimming after a small blue dinghy, on which a portable gramophone was playing a record of dance music. He had come within twenty yards, while an argent fire of phosphorescence played behind the slight wash of the boat at anchor.

The tide was making fast, the first tide of the season. Between Sharshook and Crow shingle-spit were rocky pools through which the sea pressed, swelling and overpouring onwards with many noises which together made a vast sea whisper. Boats at the estuary mouth seen from the Sharshook were tiny and far away, the crews waiting by them fragmentary black specks, sand-dissolved, moving with puny imperceptibility against a background of breakers white-crinkled under a pale blue immensity of sky.

On the crest of the Sharshook a few year-old herring gulls which had not mated were chipping off mussels from the blue clusters there, flying up, and dropping them to crack the shells. Two boat crews waited and rested below at the tide-line, a third was rowing with the current, shedding black net behind it.

Gurgling and wallowing, the Pool buoy lay in the fast water, a great rusty-red sea-top spinning on its chain.

A shout, for the rope-man on shore had seen the ream of a fish within the semi-circle of corks. Sweeps were bent as two backs straightened, rubber-booted feet braced on thwarts. Another back-fin cut the water. Tide took the boat, white above water-line and tarred beneath, licence number painted on bows, aslant its inshore direction. Iron keel-shoe grated, crew leapt out, first man flung out anchor, second man ran to help rope-man. The two couples took slow strain on the almost immovable ropes.

The skipper said, "'Tes the seven year glut." Every seventh year spring fish was plentiful. For thousands of years it had been known in the estuary village. Recently, since a century or so, hydrographers had spoken of a nine-year cycle when ocean-currents tended to set inshore. Nine years, said the scientists; seven, said the fishermen. It is the seventh wave that drowns a man, said the deep-water sailors, mast-and-yards men; and it is the seventh son of a seventh son who has power to charm salmon inshore, and he keeps his power so long as he never kills a fish, said the old women.

The fishermen hauled steadily. The tide sag-bellied the net. Water ran up and over the leaning Pool buoy. A boat which a few minutes before had been down on the South Tail moved fast up the fairway, rowed in silence over the line of corks. The skipper in the stern carried a rifle importantly across his knees. The boat was going a mile up-river, to a draught opposite the Pill, where Myxine the glutinous hag had hollowed out Petromyzon.

The boat turned north out of The String, and glided swiftly out of sight below the stones and mussel-clusters of the Sharshook.

After ten minutes the twin twenty-five fathom lengths of net, called arms, were hauled in. Remained the thirty fathom length, mid-piece, called bunt. The bunt was deeper than the arms and the meshes were smaller. Within the bunt fish were moving—the water was a-ream, uneven with bulging rises. "'Tes the zeven year glut," said the skipper. The net came easier. Wet black folds fell on the boots of the four men. Small green crabs hung on the net, menacing insignificant pincers; they fell, and were covered, struggling against new layers dropping on them. Watching, the men saw a dark brown glistening back arise and roll under. The skipper swore. A bulge of water rose and was swirled away with the tide. Faster and easier came the last of the net. They watched intently, grouped together, heel-rope men kneeling. Thresh of water, flicker, tug, boil. "Back 'er comes, boys! Steady, don't drag the seine." Never had they seen so many fish in a single draught. The netted water bubbled and splashed and shimmered.

One by one the deep-shouldered fish were lugged out by the tail, held down on net pile, and thumped on skull-base with an oaken thole-pin fetched from the boat. The skipper would never kill a fish with his own hands. He was a seventh son. He felt a calm elation. At last he was rewarded. He went for a short stroll by himself. Twenty-three fish in one draught. It was a record for the Two Rivers.

Near the Pool buoy, pulsing paired hind-flippers leisurely against the tide, Jarrk lay and chewed the twenty-fourth fish. Having eaten all he wanted, the seal sank away and drifted over the bed of the Pool, turning into the north-flowing river and rising to breathe as he passed the deep shelving slope of Crow.

Soon he came to the Creek Pool, and, bobbing up, saw a boat being rowed towards him. At the familiar sound of *Zeal!* he tipped up and swam down to the bottom, amusing himself by lying there and letting the tide take him among flatfish and crabs. He was bumping along slowly from stone to stone, the tide swilling by him with its marine litter, when Trutta the sea-trout, followed by Gralaks and six grilse, and Salar behind them, swam peacefully over him.

As Jarrk lunged upwards, the fish flashed away inshore, and so came within the hanging net. Jarrk followed them. They sank to the muddy-sand bottom, to hide. Jarrk cruised round the net, and seeing them within, rose to the surface and waited.

Seeing his blunt whiskered head by the corks, the skipper ran to the boat for the rifle, which was lying with its muzzle in the bilge. Jarrk watched while the rifle was loaded and aimed, expecting what happened: a cracking thud in the water near him, a report that raised gulls and wading birds from tide-marks far up and down the estuary; and nothing else. The seal was used to swimming down when the rifle was fired, and so he rolled under, and the marksman said this time he had hit the limmer. Some 'opes, replied his mates, watching the water as they lay back, boots sinking in wet sand, while the third man flacked the rope on the water in vain hope of scaring the seal away.

They hauled hand under hand, watching. They saw the water cut by a back-fin. Trutta, having seen Jarrk behind the net, skidded, and fled. They saw the ream of another fish, and another; a boil and jabble on the surface. Salar, Gralaks, and the grilse swimming up and down the net, seeking way of escape, had met in confusion.

The fishermen knew the heel-rope was dragging over sandy troughs and holes scoured by the previous ebb, and now being silted and rescooped by the flow. Salmon could escape in the pot-holes. So they hauled slowly, for the leaded heel-rope to conform as much as possible to the irregular bottom. Two piles of net arose slowly on rope coil and post-staffs, by their feet.

Jarrk lifted the heel-rope with head and flippers, and swam inside the net. The farthest corks were a dozen boat-lengths from the shore. The seal, his immense appetite satisfied for the moment, was playing with the fish: chasing first one, then another, rolling and blowing and tumbling. Within the net, dashing up and down to find a way out and finding none, while also fleeing in terror of meeting the seal, were Salar, Trutta, Gralaks, and six grilse. Smaller and smaller grew the arc of the net enclosing them.

The fishermen, pulling methodically, saw, an oar's length inside the corks, the leap of a grilse, and the head of the seal looking up an instant afterwards and disappearing. They swore steadily. They saw, before they had hauled three more fistfuls, a bigger salmon jump out and in and out in a series of plunging leaps along the surface, and heard the seal's teeth click behind the tail-fin. This was Salar. As they pulled less slowly, now that the weight on the ropes was not so heavy, they saw the wave of a fish approaching inshore at its greatest speed, then the boil and break of sand by their feet. "Pug!" cried the skipper, for only a large sea-trout could turn, in a few inches of water, with such invisible swiftness. They saw the ream moving back the way it had come, and the skipper shouted, "Pay off" for it was a big fish, and would strike at an angle now that the tide had carried the bunt upriver. As they dropped the ropes to slack the net, Trutta, travelling at his greatest speed, struck the mesh with his nose, and drave through.

Only dabs, seaweed, and crabs were in the seine when it was lifted ashore, to be picked up and looked at. The mesh twine was new; a single strand could not be broken by a steady pull between a man's hands. The sea-trout had broken nine meshes, and through the rent all the fish had escaped.

BOOK TWO

Book Two:
Spring Spate

7 Tide-Head

Rain fell from grey clouds over the estuary at floodtide, and Salar leapt for the change in the water. From the hills, clouds in close pack could be seen apparently following the valley which was the estuary; but this was condensation in the colder, windy air above water. Wind from the south-west pressed skits on the waves, and the rain spread to the hills and the moor, and by nightfall every drain and runner and ditch was noisy with falling water. Through pipe and culvert and chute the water hurried, with its differing loads, matter inanimate and suspended, dead leaves, soil, tar-acids from the broken surface of second-class roads, oil, decaying things, and the gases arisen from the disturbance of mud in eddies of the river and its influent streams. Rain poured from a sky without star or moon but luminously stained by the lights of the town under whose ancient bridge the ebb moved heavily and swiftly to the river's mouth: thickly the tide ebbed, overpressed and overweighted by the volume of the spate.

There was no fishing from gravel ridge or sandbank that night. Old tree trunks and roots rode down in the grey-brown water. Far out in the bay the sea was distained when daylight came. The landscape was dissolved in falling grey rain.

Salar had gone up under the familiar piers of the Long Bridge the night before, but, meeting the freshet's thrust, he had turned aside to avoid the thick-water irritations in his gillrakers. Under the stone wall of the quay there was an eddy of salt water, where with other salmon he rested; but the rising turbid volume of road and field washings swept the eddy away, and the fish turned and swam towards the sea. They gulped unevenly in water which, saturated with carbonic acid gas released from rotting vegetation and silt in ditches and pool eddies, was additionally acid with peat-water run from bog-plashes of the moor. Soon this brown opaque water, loaded with leaves and sticks, was absorbed in the wider waters of the estuary; and into the half-ebb Salar turned, to move across the currents until he found a good stream. Other fish moved with him.

Forward into this they felt their way, turning instantly as they ran into a layer of water which caused them to gulp with choking. This water had been cutting into the mud banks of rotted turf overlaid with sludge below the town's open sewer in the quay wall. Avoiding its acrid taints, Salar found the clearer and faster streams of the secondary freshet which now was coming down. There were no tar-acids or oil-scums in this wide and pleasant water, although leaf-fragments and black twigs were moving thickly over the bed of the fairway. It was runnable water, and he leapt, and drove quickly against its exhilarations. Finding that the good stream continued and broadened, he sought slower water by the edge of sandbank and salting, and moved up faster, but always at the verge of the main or parent stream.

Salar had moved up through this channel many times during the moon's wax and wane; he had drifted with the water, letting the tide take him, slower and slower, until the tidal pool was reached. Here fresh water had lain over the heavier salt, stagnant, chilling, brackish. Roots of trees and rocky juts were slimy with fine mud suspended and settled in the lifeless lake. Disillusioned, he had drifted back with surface flotsam and wreckage and froth which began to return the instant it reached the tide-head; every time the tide-head water had moved back without pause, waveless, assoiled, Salar with it.

But now the stream was alive, and he took life from it. This water was coloured, but not turbid. It was the spate fining down after the first load of drain water had carried away stagnant deposits of used life awaiting recreation. It was not yet water springing from the rock, but it was water enlivened by percussion and repercussion against the living rock and air of earth. A million million bubbles of air had been beaten into it by the force of gravity, a million million fragments of rock had dragged against and resisted its momentum; every swirl and tear and crashing fall had been attended by watchful air. It was saturated with oxygen, sparkling water, life-giving water, faithful to the spirit of Salmon. It was grand running water, and the fish leapt to it, fleeing fast after shadowy companions in play, and, as the spirit sank in them after its exaltation, boring steadily onwards again.

Salar passed under a railway bridge, its tubular iron pillars ringed by marks of old tides. Above, the river ran under sloping banks of mud, gliddery stuff, frittered by castings of rag-worms which had their vertical tunnels deep in black sand beneath the mud. This sand was black with the carbon of ancient oak-leaves and twigs and turf covered by salt of tides after the sea-wall had been raised to reclaim marshland otherwise drowned by every spring-tide. At low tide draining water from the marsh gushed through wooden traps hinged above the culverts opening under the wall; the pressure of high tide kept the traps closed, and behind them the water accumulated until the tidal level dropped.

Enclosed and dociled within grassy walls, the river wound eel-like through the marsh. Soon Salar was passing under another railway bridge. He slid forward by a pillar against which the stream was divided and flung out, causing underwater recoil. He was lifted up and back, but swam out of the turbulence, which would have drowned a powerful human swimmer, with three easy sinuations.

The smooth sandy bottom of the estuary was left behind. The waterflow was torn by rocks and boulders of angular and linear shape. They lay between the sea's abrasiveness and the river's smaller polishing. Seaweed grew poorly on the lumps of rock, fretted by alien silt during tidal flows and then swilled by enervating saltless water: enduring alien air while awaiting the sea's brief benison twice every day. And because it was broken water, mud-streaming, unrhythmic, Salar ceased his leaping. To avoid bruise and jar, constantly he had to rise, to swing sideways, to pause and waver before feeling a way around sharp rocks and the rough higgledy-piggledies of the formless watercourse. It was hybrid of sea and river; it was artificial, man-altered, unnatural. The water spirit did not dwell there: its laws and verities were changed and obstructed. Like all hybrids, it was unproductive, outside its cycle established in the great orbit of the sun. The life it created and nourished—except the rag-worms which were there temporarily—mullet, bass, flatfish, eels, and shrimps, was tidal-transient. One day the deposits of carbonized leaves and turf, on which the worms fed, would be tunnelled through, assimilated, refined as silt and raised to the surface as castings; then the worms would perish. It was negative land and negative water, belonging not to composition or life, but to dissolution and death.

Salmon, stream-shapen and wave-wrought, were made uneasy, fatigued, in the pill or creek at low water. Many injured themselves, bruising skin and flesh as they hastened to pass through the area. Salar had journeyed here many times before, but always on the flowing tide, in water a fathom deep and more. But this was fresh water rushing in spate over a bed silted by the slower, lesser streams of more than a hundred days.

A small trout was washed past Salar, belly upwards, poisoned by gas bursting suddenly out of a black wad of old leaves in the eddy where it had been resting. Only a small part of the gas had been absorbed as the bubbles wriggled upwards, but it was enough to poison the fish after three gulps.

Salar pressed on, although discomforted and gill-stung, because the water cleared as he went forward. He swam around the wider bends, where the current was less strong, and where usually an eddy moved against the main direction of the river. By the roots of the first oak, a massive tree growing in knotted strength out of rock bared cliff-like by a streamlet entering the creek, he rested, hovering near the surface to avoid the silt-drag below.

While he was hovering there he saw a form move beside him which made him turn and swim away at his fastest speed. The form was seal-like, and slightly smaller than himself, but he recognized it instantly as an enemy. This was a young otter, which had been equally startled to see so large an object appear beside it. The otter had come down to play in the water after hunting rabbits in the hillside oakwood; for during a spate it could not hunt in water. Realizing, after the thudding shock of Salar's acceleration, that it was fish, the otter began to hunt around the ledges of rock in which the oak's roots were grown, hoping to surprise fish there. And, groping and peering, the otter came face to face with Trutta the sea-trout, who immediately drove past the otter and knocked it sprawling. Trutta had met otters before, and knew them for slow swimmers who could not hurt him unless they got him into shallow water.

Searching the bed of the eddy, where water turned against shillets at the base of the rocky wall, the otter came upon a smaller fish which was resting there, cowed by the presence of a small river-lamprey which was eating into its side. The fish was one of the six grilse which had travelled from the Island Race with Gralaks at the full of the moon. The grilse was cowering there, its body curved and taut. The otter sprang sideways off webbed hind-feet with a sweep of its thick tail and as the grilse started off its snapping teeth bit the lamprey, pulling it away from the fish's flank. Swimming up, the young otter crawled out along a root and began to eat the lamprey tail-first, as it had eaten eels with its mother and fellow-cubs during the eel-migration of the previous fall. The taste of the lamprey was unfamiliar, and the otter left it, departing into the wood again to hunt rabbits. Shore rats found the lamprey later, and ate it up.

Meantime Salar had gone up the river, which ran slower

through a long pit with rocky side and bottom under the oakwood. Now the water was running slower and clearer, and he swam comfortably through a regular surge of water. The opposite bank was walled, but rough marshy ground was giving way to grassy pasture. Here the first alder grew; the true river was not far away, for alders cannot grow near salt–water.

So Salar came at last to the natural river, where it wound widely and was allowed to make its own pools and backwaters, to cut into its ancient bed and form its own islets. Its gravel was clean and its music was sharp after the sombrous rhythms of the sea.

8 *Valley of Oakwoods*

Trutta moved over the shillets where water was slow and unbroken. The shillets were flat fragments of rock, not yet ground to gravel, lying below the pools which had been cut out of the bends above. During a spate every part of the river bottom, except bedrock, was in movement, however gradual; and where the stream slowed the shillets and gravel slowed, and accumulated. At every bend Salar avoided deep and fast water, but kept to its edge, moving steadily upstream. Trutta followed.

A dark stain was slowly deepening on the sea-trout's head, on the back of his neck and behind the gill-covers. His dorsal fin was torn and scales on his back were scraped off. He was a sick fish, and Salar was piloting him. Salar was unaware of Trutta's weakness and pain, but he knew he was being followed, and was content thereby. His tail was guarded. Also he knew Trutta for something like himself, a familiar form accompanying his life, making the same journey.

The sea-trout was using Salar's sense of direction for himself; he was weary, desirous of reaching the Junction Pool, where he might trust himself to the river and rest. He ached along his entire body. The shock of breaking through the net had injured the nervous tissue between brain and the balancing levels in his head. These water-levels were three in number, two of them vertical and at right angles one to another, the third was horizontal. Sometimes Trutta lurched sideways, losing his balance. This made him fearful, and so he followed Salar, keeping just behind the salmon's tail.

At mirk midnight Salar moved up the river as easily as he had moved when the sun was high. He felt his way, as he was swimming, through the varying pressures of the stream. Currents and wedges and back-lies of water were being formed and shaped by every ledge of rock and boulder in the river; each rock and boulder was thereby sensed before it was encountered. Every moment the salmon, through the linked nerve-cells down his sides, was adjusting himself automatically to the different flumes and countering swirls which were as vibrations or little shocks: rock and stone echoes in fluid motion about him. He did not need the sense of sight; but Trutta, dismayed and sick, the automatic balance and levels of his brain upset, was travelling by sight, following Salar's tail.

Salar avoided the deep rushing water of the main stream. Sometimes he moved in water scarcely deep enough to cover his back-fin, water streaming fast over gravel banks thrown up on inner bends of the river's course, usually below pools. These gravel beds remained there because the water-force was not sufficient to shift them. The river bed was always moving, even at low summer level, when perhaps only grains of sand were stirring. The sand accumulated behind a small stone, forming a tiny scour which as it increased altered the echo-set of its flumes, which in turn disturbed and swirled other particles of gravel. A piece of stone as big as a man's fist, suddenly shifting, caused disturbance or rearrangement over an area many times its size. But when the river was in spate its cutting powers were increased a millionfold. Every snag lodging temporarily against a rock caused the beginning of movement in a thousand pebbles and shillets; and with every movement they were diminished, chipped, ground, rubbed, and abraded. Every river and stream was helping to cut through the world.

Stray seeds, washed down and lodged on gravel banks below bends, sprouted and grew in summer, many of them enduring winter floods to grow in glory of air and sun during their second and final summer. Salar swam over plants low on the gravel, tansy, soapwort, hemlock, water-celery, and silver-weed. Among them were brown stalks of docks, relics of last summer's greenery, and against these stalks, some broken off and others bent, dead leaves and loose water-weed and twigs were fixed by the water-flow. The docks put down a deep tap-root into the gravel and flourished there many seasons.

Salar swam by roots binding themselves into the rock of a mid-stream island, and came to a weir which was built diagonally across the river. Under the weir the water was harsh and white. Followed by Trutta, he felt a way across the spread of little water, seeking the power of the main stream. The other end of the weir was built into a second island, and after putting his nose hesitatingly into the fussy shallow water below the apron of the weir, he rested in the eddy of the island-end.

The weir had been built in another century to dam the river and

Michael J. Loates

so to store water for the working of a mill. Beyond the end of the weir a salmon trap had been made. This was a narrow channel, faced and floor'd with stone to prevent cutting-away by fast water when in use. The water passing through could be regulated, and stopped altogether, by sliding fenders or doors.

In the days of the trap's usage, before the Conservancy Board had bought out the rights, salmon were taken this way. During a freshet, when fish were running, the upper fender was lifted a couple of feet, and water gushed through at great pressure from the deep mill-pool above. The lower fender was opened wide, so that fish, reluctant to ascend the white slopes of the weir, would find an easy and secure way under it. But when they got to the upper fender, and attempted to explore the strength and direction of the constricted water before launching themselves into it, invariably they were forced back. So they waited under the wall, in eddies and secondary streams, for the pressure of water to lessen. Soon many fish were resting there.

Then the weir-keeper and his assistant dropped the fenders, the salmon were netted out, knocked on the head with a small lead-weighted bludgeon called a priest, and sent to market. In a good season the riparian owner made several hundred pounds out of his salmon trap.

Before the Board of Conservators was formed for the protection and maintenance of the stock of salmon and trout of the Two Rivers, there were many weirs and traps obstructing the free running of these fish. Very few salmon reached the spawning redds of the head-waters of the river. Every weir was an obstacle; and there were frequent weirs, damming the river for the water to turn the wheels of mill-houses. The invention of the steam-engine was indirectly the cause of much pollution of rivers, and the consequent destruction of river-life; and it was also the indirect cause of the general dereliction of water-mills. When Salar and Gralaks and Trutta were born, most of the weirs which had stopped their ancestors from journeying up the river, except in the big floods, were washed out. The fish-traps were ruinous, too.

Salar, followed by Trutta, found an easy way up fast and deep water pouring past the mossy posts of the fenders which long since had decayed. They entered a slow, heavy pool, with a muddy bottom, and swam up under the right bank, against the flow swinging and wimpling about the roots of oaks and alders. They passed submerged rocks on which grass was flattened, and willow withies swayed bending, stemming the flood with loads of dead leaves and twigs.

Salar rested in front of a willowy lodge, maintaining himself in the cushion of water in rebound from the rock.

Something behind him glimmered strangely, as with moonlight. He tried to approach it by rising in the water, when it vanished, since it was then beyond his cone of vision. Other fish had seen the glimmer, and waited beside the rock, in the riffle it caused in the stream, attracted to the light. It was the corpse of a kelt which had died of exhaustion and fungus disease a month before. It was held in the withies. Broken, its skin torn and most of the scales stripped, it was glowing with the phosphoric fires of ocean, the last of its life-flame burning out.

The fish watching and rising to the light were curious; it was a fixed object, their curiosity was for movement, and so they passed on.

Salar came to another ruined weir, over the foundations of which the river pushed, determined to wash the last traces of man's work from its course. Rows of wooden posts driven into the gravel slanted across the river, battered and gnawn by the water and the life it nourished and held. The weir had been made of oaken posts and planks filled with shillets; but one day the river had worked its way through one small place, and everlastingly had pushed through the crevice, shifting first one small gravel speck, then another little stone, and at last had cleared a way between the lowest plank and the bedrock. Wider the way was cleared, and the smaller the river in summer drought the greater the pressure of water gushing through, sweeping the pit under the weir and cutting out gravel packed around the posts, until one day a freshet swilling down the river had burst a way through, and the millpool, with its thousands of tons of silt and snags and eels, went rushing down the river.

Now alders and willows, which had been brought down in old floods, were rooted behind the posts, causing the high water to pour over and beside the clumps of their roots and accumulations of leaves and twigs lodged there, and to swirl about the posts, thus slowly washing away the gravel in which they were bedded.

Salar rested in the deep pit still remaining on one side of the weir, and then swam up between two posts, and past a much-polled willow, followed by Trutta. As they moved into the slower and deeper flow under the farther bank, they felt weighted shakings in the water, and sped up fast, fearing an enemy, and came to watchful rest upstream under a shelf of rock. The cause of their alarm was a train passing, for the railway here lay beside the river.

Since they had swum through the long Carrion Pit below the

oakwood, the water had been dropping back under the river banks, but now it was rising again, and thickening with colour of the fields. Very few of these fields were under the plough, although they were rich for corn; first the mills declined with the general use of the steam-engine; then the price of corn, due to the steam-engine in ships which brought grain cheaply from the great plains of America, fell below the cost of its cultivation. The riverside cornlands were now pasture for sheep and cattle, and thus the ditches between them drained water less turbid than in the storm of a previous century. Also the draining of swamps and marshes and roads caused the surface water to run away more rapidly, and so the spates rose and fell quickly.

As the river was rising Salar moved on, to find a seat where he might rest safe from surprise and near deep water if so he needed to escape from an enemy. He came to a rock, swung about behind it, and swam on exploring; then he drifted backwards and settled in the riffle of water below the rock. The edge of the fast water gripped him comfortably, and maintained him with the least effort; so that the sea-lice on his body, which had been growing more and more agitated since their host had entered fresh water, hung inert in sleep.

Salar lay contentedly, for the wound in his side had ceased to ache, while the fast stream passed an inch off his nose—at the last startle of danger he could get to safe water.

Innumerable salmon, during many centuries, had been caught on flies of feather and steel and silk while idling behind that small mid-river rock, taking stray nymphs swimming by. From father to son that salmon lodge had been known, and in later ages, tenants of the fishing beat learned of it; poachers knew it; herons, flying slowly over in summer weather when the river was low and clear, were used to seeing a salmon dawdling there. At low summer level the top of the rock was streaked white, and small-splotched with greenish-black scriddicks of fish-bones, the spraints of otters. The rock, owing to the position of ledges in the river-bed above it, was at the tail of a pool and at all heights of water in the fairway, was a rest for salmon, a touching place for otters, a stance for herons.

Salar rested behind the rock, and soon another salmon was resting there also, and then a third salmon; since lodges were occupied by a varying number of fish when they were running. The salmon lay behind and beside Salar, knowing of one another without sight in the roaring water-darkness. More fish moved into the rock's riffled after-quiet, sheltering from fine sand now moving generally in the river—for the second fresh was disturbing the fine gravel-scours deposited by the spate in decline—which hurt their gills. Soon salmon were lying side by side and touching, and in four layers, one above the other. Behind the rear fish lay Trutta, and beside him was a kelt, a slender fish with new sharp teeth, which had been going tail-first down-river when it met the first clean-run fish, and there-upon became much excited, and began to travel upstream with them. It had eaten five trout since meeting the new salmon. This fish was what rod-and-line fishermen called a well-mended kelt, because it had the silvery appearance of a fish new from the sea although it was thin. They said a kelt mended itself, that it changed from river-brown, the tarnish and dislustre of stagnation, to an argentine anticipation of ocean: and how it mended itself, they declared, whether or not it fed during or after its perlustration, was a mystery, like the primal sea-change of smolts while yet in the river. The bright deposit was an armour against corrosion, a temper for brine-weighted water, and it was made from an excretion of the body, a waste-product, a kind of solder sweated on each scale. Thus the kelt, exhausted salmon, was reborn; its sharp teeth and bright scales were a death-desperate hope of resurrection.

Salmon new from the Atlantic had few teeth in their mouths, for their teeth had worn and dropped out, and they needed none when their bodies were full-stored for the ascension of their rivers.

The kelt's silveriness had come rapidly, made by guanin, excretion from its flaccid stomach. When it had begun to feed again, the chemicals of indigestion were generated, and thereby were its scales sweated bright. Those scales were much broken at the edges: serrated.

The kelt lay beside Trutta, and Trutta lay beside Gralaks the grilse, and the water rose higher until there was a phalanx of salmon behind the rock. Heavier fell the rain and soon the river was over its banks and bending the lower branches of alders which in summer would bear masses of sticks and leaves like old bird-nests many feet above the river.

A tree came lurching and bumping down-river, and struck the rock and scattered the fish sideways into the current and then down-stream. They turned again to bore into and get the weight and feel of the water against their flanks. Unsure of himself, Salar swam across the stream until he was under the left bank, where the rush of water was slowed down against alder branches.

He did not remain there long, because he was unsure of a way of retreat, having come across the main stream; so he worked forward until he was clear of the branches and in deep water that moved slowly. It moved over reeds which bended palely to its flow. Various wildfowl were feeding here, and Salar saw them above him, for some of their feathers and feather-reflections were fluorescent in the darkness. This was in ordinary times a back-water, lying in an old bed which the river, ever cutting stone from stone under its banks, had deserted—for a while: since all the level valley was old river-bed, gradually being discovered and recovered by water falling between hills to the sea.

Salar, liking the quiet steadiness of the water flowing there, nosed forward into the stream. Very soon it ran fast and shallow, over its olden bed which was now an irregular part of a field. He swam up, over flattened grasses and nettle clumps whose yellow roots were stringing from the stones. He was swept back, and rested behind the nettle clump, in surging water, holding to a stone with his pectoral fins. A pink flat-headed lob-worm, dug out by the water, was swept past him, and he opened his mouth, sucked it in, and crushed it between tongue and vomer, swallowing it.

Then, feeling that the force of the water was lessening, and being more confident of the way, he swam up strongly and reached calmer water which was revolving in a pit below the roots of an oak-stump pushed there during a greater spate two winters ago. He rested awhile, his left flank swept by the twisting roll of water, which kept him almost immobile, except for an occasional flexion of the body, against the gravelly upsurge in the pit. Soon he was joined by Trutta, followed by Gralaks, and the slim kelt.

9 *Clear Water*

Salar had been resting in the pit for a short while when he realized that the water was falling less. He pressed forward into the wide and shallow rush above the tree stump. There he lay awhile, exhilarated by the water, which was ringing with bubbles of oxygen. He knew the way back, and lay there enjoying the keen and tingling feel of the water as it prepared to sweep up and over and around the trunk. His tail played gently with the playful water.

The stump was massive. For years it had been travelling down the river, after being washed out of the river bank above the Fireplay Pool. Five centuries the oak had grown there, in its maturity leaning mossy, fern-clad, and massive over the water. Its summer leaves were shady; in them mingled the songs of air and water. Wild duck had laid their eggs in the folds of its lower branches, water-ousels hung their water-moss nests in holes of its trunk overhanging the stream. Yellow wagtails nested there too, and little brown wrens, and dimmit-flitting water-bats. Otters sometimes lay sunning themselves along its boughs, watching the shadow-play of leaves on the gravel below; herons perched among its topmost branches and surveyed the surrounding land for human enemies before gliding down to fish at the tail of the Fireplay; voles and moorhens walked under its water-side roots, through which the winter spates pressed, carving the brown bank under. The tree stood, or leaned, year after year, unmoved by the power of water, for its main roots were far into the parkland through which the river ran. But one day an old man died; and many of his trees died with him, felled to pay death-duties to the state. For scores of years after its trunk had been made into gate-posts, furniture, and coffin boards, the irregularly circular base of the tree remained in the river bank while dry-rot ate the hidden roots away, and at last it fell into the water and was shifted down the river by freshets, lodging against rocks and in eddies until a heavy spate

became a flood over water-meadows and fields and it was taken
down the valley as though it were one of its old leaves.

Now it was lodged in the old river bed, near the place where its
parent tree had stood nearly a thousand years before. A wood dove,
having swallowed some of the parent tree's acorns, had flown up the
valley, to be seen by Chakchek the Smiter, whose talon-stroke ripped
open its crop. The acorn had fallen to the bank above the pool, and in
the following spring had put down its tap-root among the grasses.

There is a graveyard of ancient oaks by the South Tail of the
estuary of the Two Rivers, trees drowned by sea and buried in sand
before the Danes' galleys sailed in from the west; when the wolf
howled under the moon, and the sabre-toothed tiger strode low and
tense upon moose and elk and red deer of the forest. The stumps and
roots are now brown coal in the sand under the beat of Atlantic
rollers, with flint arrowheads, and bones and skulls of men and
animals. Here on coloured ebb-tides the uprooted trees of the river are
borne, carried out to sea and returned on calmer waters, to lie sodden
in the sand, with their ancestors beyond leaf-memory of sun or star.

Above the tree stump Salar lay, enjoying rich breathing in a
muse of himself, until the tree root shifted, and he became aware of
shoaling water. He swam strongly forward into a fast racing stream,
feeling his dorsal and tail fins in air. This scared him, and he swam
with all his strength, tearing the water; Trutta followed him, not so
alarmed, for the sea-trout was used to travelling in shallow water by
night. The two fish came to a shallow pit smoothed with grass, at the
bottom of which the water was moving in a direction opposite to the
tangled surface flow. Salar followed up the main flow barrelling along
at the sides of the inverted eddy, and entered an area of shifting shillets
and sand-streaming rapid water, from which he turned, and, going
back to the grassy pit, he rested his pectoral fins on the drowned grass
and idled there at rest. Trutta lay beside Salar, but not on his pectoral
fins, which were narrower and not so strong.

The level of the water was sinking rapidly. It was a freshet from
the valley of one of the tributary streams, a temporary head of
rainwater from a cloudburst above hillsides of scrub-oak. Trutta
began to rove round the pit. The old sea-trout knew the river, having
returned to it from the sea seven times before; but he did not recognize
this place, and he was uneasy.

His uneasiness was given to Salar, who prepared to swim up the
rough slide from which he had already turned back. He cruised round
the pit against the roll of water and made a half-leap, showing head

and back and tail above water, and then swimming down again he sought the main rush and bored upwards into it. Trutta followed him after a short interval. The sea-trout was used to swimming through stickles—rough stony shallows—working a way from stone to stone; but Salar lost his nerve. He struck himself against large stones in his efforts to get quickly to safety. Four of his sea-lice were crushed, and fell away with some of his scales. These parasites were already sick, and for some hours previously had ceased in feebleness to suck Salar's blood.

He reached a stretch of rippling shallow through which he could move only by the most violent threshing of the water. He lost himself in fear, and drove into a stone, striking his head, and lay on his side, washed by the water. Then with a sweep of his tail he turned downstream to the pit and continued through it past the oak stump and so to the deeper water whither Trutta had already returned. Another salmon which had been moving doubtfully up the side-stream turned when it met him, and then swung round again, to drop back slowly, tail-first, with the current.

The fish remained in the pool whereon the wild-fowl were splashing and feeding until the flow from the old river bed ceased, when they turned away and sought the main stream. This was swift and deep and narrow under brown cliffs of meadow land which it was fast undercutting. Salar worked across the main stream to the edge of its swiftness, swimming in water less than two feet deep, and over many small green plants of balsam which had sprouted from seeds lying since last summer in the gravel.

The balsam plant in summer was as tall as a man, a hollow red stem filled with liquid, and bearing amidst its narrow leaves clusters of pink and white flowers becoming, after pollination by bees, pods which on a hot sunny day catapulted their seeds several yards with distinct snapping noises. This ingenious method of assuring its immortality had planted many millions of offspring along scores of miles of river bank since a single plant had started to spread itself from a cottage garden half a century previously.

Rain fell no more, the air lightened with the last of the clouds dragging away into the north-east and the high hills of the moor. Stars shone, the wind was warm. There was release in air and water; owls hooted softly with pleasure in the spruce-fir plantations of the valley sides; foxes shook their coats and flaired the wind; rabbits lolloped and paused, ears lifted, lolloped on and paused before settling to nibble new grass around their forepaws; salmon half-leapt as they left eddy

Whitefield Barton looking
to Challacombe Common
Michael J. Loates

and lie and moved into the broad flow of the river.

Salar swam with quiet ease, watchful yet trusting himself to the greatness of the river. Mud and soil were gone from the water, which now was almost clear for fish; although to human eyes, were it daylight, the river would have appeared fawn-brown in colour, opaque. Rapidly the spate was fining down, depositing sand and leaf-fragments, borne in its myriad mingled streams, by its myriad eddies and pockets. On wet branches of bankside alders and oaks dripping platforms of stalks of bramble and rush and tree sticks were lodged with torn water-weed and other cast flotsam—rusty cans and medicine bottles and hens' feathers from valley farmhouses—and an occasional green ivy spray torn away by the south-west gale.

The river moved with immense power, irresistible yet confined. Its tortuous volume held many deep sounds of rock resistance, lesser noises of gravel movement—defeated rock—and the protests of water against tree trunks and branches. By the air most of these sounds were unheard. The air was free of its conflict with water, it flowed with its own life unconfined, a free element; and to the air the salmon, embodied spirit of water, leapt in joy of freedom.

Over the moor the young moon arose with the morning star, and water everywhere rejoiced in their light. Raindrops on thorns and lichens of the moor glinted, hill trickles and rillets ran gleaming threads, odd slates on farmhouse roofs were ashine, each tree branch carried a thin line of light, the broad river was silver-splayed. *Krark* cried Old Nog the heron flying darkly over, his eye glinting.

When the sun rose Salar was resting behind one of the columnar piers of a railway bridge crossing the river. After a while he drifted backwards and rested at the tail of the pool because rain-water dripping from the bridge was acrid. Twenty-four jackdaws perching in a row on the iron parapet were croaking unhappily one to another, for their nesting hopes had been checked by the recent tarring of the steel framework. The railway workmen had thrown into the river nearly a hundredweight of old sticks.

A drowned black-faced lamb with legs and head hanging below its body floated under the bridge, revolving with the swirls of the stream. It had fallen off a boulder on the granite moor where it had played with other lambs in the cold sunny weather of its eight weeks of life. Often it had jumped, all four legs at once, and with flourish of long tail, across the river; for the river there was only a short way from its source in the morass where five rivers began. But when the rain had been falling an hour the rivulet was roaring big, and the lamb either did not heed or did not hear the low *baa-aa* of warning, and slipping, was carried away, bumped and hurled over other boulders and rocks until its cries were lost in water. Yet the ewe heard them still as she ran and leapt in distress down the valley, the sight of her causing other black-faced ewes to stand and stare and knock their front hoofs with alarm. The ewe ran down the valley calling her lamb.

Salar saw head and legs before him, and imagining otter, sped away across the river, sinking under the opposite bank where other fish, with Trutta and the kelt, were resting. His coming alarmed them and they turned and swam downstream. The lamb was borne away in the surging water, and soon they forgot their alarm and returned to their places; scarcely heeding the shape of the ewe floating over them; for it was on its back, legs in air.

10 *Junction Pool*

By noon Salar had travelled under two more railway bridges and one road bridge and come to a deep and wide pool above an elongated islet on which trees were growing. This was the Junction Pool. Its width and depth were carved by another river flowing into the main river at right angles.

The islet, a haunt of otters, had been formed when the railway was made in the valley nearly a century before. A bridge on steel columns filled with concrete was built across the main river fifty yards above the Junction Pool, where it was gravelly and shallow. Soon winter spates, pressing against and around the obstructing columns, had scooped all gravel off the rock and carried the gravel down into the Junction Pool. This new gravel-bed altered the set of the streams in the pool; and these streams began to cut it away at once, spates swirled the loose stones and shillets and dropped them in the first slack water. So a ridge was raised, narrow and streamlined. Water-celery plants, docks, nettles, balsam helped to bind the gravel. Seeds of alder and willow sprouted in its compost of dead leaves. It became an islet. Every flood raised it, silting its vegetation, leaving piles of sticks and leaves against its trees. The sticks and leaves rotted, a more luxuriant vegetation arose.

In that time before the railway was built, before the new pool was carved below the piers of the bridge, most fish ascending from the sea passed through the stronger and more direct stream of the large river and so came eventually to the headwaters in the green and granite moor. Now the larger river flowed deep, sluggish, uninviting. The lesser stream from the side valley rushed in fast, with its song of clean gravel. Thus the majority of salmon and sea-trout, after resting in the Junction Pool, turned north and entered the smaller but keener stream, coming at last to the spawning redds under the moor of the red deer.

Between the two moors were small valleys and hills divided by banks and hedges into scores of thousands of small fields. Some of these fields, called splatts, were so small that the potatoes they grew would hardly feed one man in a season. Most of them were rough grazing, and very few were larger than ten acres. They lay between boggy tracts with scanty sheep-bite on them, where curlews, plover, snipe, and wild duck nested, and wildered thorns were grey with lichens and shaggy with green moss. It was a high country of winds and rains, glowing before twilight with stupendous Atlantic sunsets. From this land, watered by the distillations of ocean, the river drew its being.

A litter of sticks and leaves lay on the broken edge of the meadow north of the islet, marking the nocturnal height of the spate. The banks of the meadow were sheer, cliff-like, for the water between islet and mainland ran swift and gliding there, undercutting the field.

From the smaller river the stream swept in, to be pushed and

Michael J. Loates 1984

deflected by the slower, heavier water flowing from under the railway bridge. After certain confusions, the combined waters began to move off together, but almost immediately they divided into two fast runs past the islet.

The inflowing stream was elephant-grey, waving and swinging ponderously, slowing deliberately as it swung across the pool, there to curl upon itself with innumerable whirls and irregular sudden expansions and reversions of water. That was the tail of the run, the eddy; and there the salmon lay, a contented and loose formation of fish, some on the bed of the river or in mid-water, while others were poised on the edge of back-trends apparently broadside on to the flow of the river.

The varying movements and weights of flowing water maintained various movements and weights of fish. Slower, heavier salmon, which had been in the estuary for weeks, a coppery tinge on their scales of dull silver, lay in slower, deeper water. Salar was among them. With other large spring salmon he was lying over weed-waving stones on the edge of rapid water, just clear of the eddy-tail, above the islet.

Gralaks and six grilse, forerunners of the main shoals of grilse which would enter the river at midsummer, swam near the surface. Sometimes one rose easily and half-lobbed itself out of the water and sank down to its place in the formation.

A school of small spring fish lay beside the heavier salmon, but in the quick water gliding past the islet. These fish weighed about nine pounds each; but one was a pound lighter, and one was almost twelve pounds. They had left the river two years before as smolts, weighing about two and a half ounces each, but one had been slightly smaller than the others, and the other weighed three ounces. They had roamed the sea together and come into the estuary on the flowing tide following the ebb into which Salar had run. They had travelled fast and in great zest of the oxygen in the river, and leaping continually, all the way from the Island Race to the Junction Pool in less than forty-eight hours. They were keen in pride and strength of the sea, their backs bluish like new-cut lead, while their flanks were a soft whitish silver, or rather the hue of tin, which of olden time was mined and streamed in all the rivers of the granite moor. It is a purer and more lustrous metal than silver.

The small spring fish, which had just entered the Junction Pool, were assured and confident. They had come direct from the ocean, finding the water of their parent river immediately in the Island Race.

Indeed the sea was stained for several miles beyond the Bell Buoy with brown flood-water. In the estuary they had encountered neither seal nor net; they had run straight through on the tide. These salmon lay in swift water because its swiftness was their own.

Trutta the sea-trout had pushed himself under some alder roots growing matted along the left bank, one of his homes, and there he lay, asleep, oblivious of all river life, even his own, yet automatically ready to move alive should the retina of his eye, or the nerve-cells of his lateral line, be affected by alien movement.

Small brown trout, each having its hiding hole under bank or root or stone, were lying everywhere on the gravel except in the fastest runs. They were watching for food, displaced nymphs and stone-fly creepers, to move near them.

A shoal of resident dace, pink-finned, lay in characterless water near the old sea-trout, idly waiting for drowned worms and insects to drift into the pit.

The kelt, long-headed and lean, ravaged of spirit and consumed of body, its gills hung with maggots and its scales broken-edged, roved round the Junction Pool, unable to rest, gigantic disillusioned smolt, in search of a scattered identity. It lay awhile behind Salar, imitating his complacency; then wriggled upwards to Gralaks and her companion grilse, and sinuated quickly with the movement of young fish. Gralaks swam up slowly and leapt in a low curve; the kelt swam up too quickly, rose on its frayed tail-fin, and fell back with a splash that made the seagulls, fleeing crook-winged in the wind over the valley, to wheel and slant down, uttering cadaver-cries of wild in-human ocean.

The hovering indifference of the grilse set the kelt roving again round the pool. He lay behind a stone by the clean-cut fish in the throat of the glide; they shifted diagonally, keeping their formation. He was longer than Salar and yet less thick than one of the small springers. The water of the glide was too strong for the kelt, and he wriggled up to the trough of the Pool.

Gradually the air was growing less cold in the valley. The wind eddied slower, warmer. Sunshine heated the opening buds of alders and for a while their lichened branches steamed slightly, with iridescence, then invisibly. A spider drew itself from shelter behind loose dead bark, walked into the sun-rays, rested and warmed itself, moved as a branch-shadow moved; and towards noon, with sudden elation, threw a gossamer into the air. It gleamed red and blue as it drifted twisting. Other gossamers were floating. They were signals of the air's buoyancy. Water was absorbing oxygen rapidly.

And of a sudden, as though they had been awaiting a signal, all the salmon in the pool began to move, slowly at first, cruising just under the surface; then accelerating, one after another they leapt at the air. Far up and down the river, in the tails of pools and from the braided edges of the eddies, mile upon mile of grey swilling water broke with splashes.

Not only was the spirit released in fish, but also in smaller forms of water life. Nymphs of the olive dun, which since hatching from eggs the summer before had lived under stones and among the dark green fronds of water-moss, were now leaving the element of water for the element of air. They were swimming to the surface, breaking their confining nymphal skins, and, having unfolded and dried their new wings as they rode down on the water, were rising into the hymenal brightness of the sky. Trout and salmon parr shifted into the eddies, watching forward and upwards, rising to suck them into their mouths. The larger parr, most of them two years old, were already assuming the silvery sheen of smolthood. They fed eagerly, swimming up faster than trout of the same size, in their vehemence sometimes leaping out of the water. Those on the gravel, amidst salmon at pause in their sporting, appeared to vibrate with eagerness while waiting to turn on their sides to take the nymphs leaving their shelters.

Salar, having cruised round the pool, showing back and fin thrice above water, leapt and returned to his place. He saw above and below him gleams of small fish as they half-rolled to take nymphs. He saw larger gleams, the half-rolls of Gralaks and other grilse as they opened their mouths to do the same. Salar began to take them too. He was not hungry: he was stimulated by rich breathing, excited by parr-memory and joyous river-life come again, disporting himself.

The kelt took a smolt that flashed before him, sank down holding it crosswise in his jaws, while its body writhed deeper into the sharp teeth; and when it was still he turned it head-first on his tongue, and gorged it.

Some of the duns hatched, and flew slowly up on pale wings, to cling to branches and twigs of alder in frail wonder of the new world of air and light.

The kelt leapt and fell back formlessly with a furrowed splash. From on high as they straggled over the hill on their way to known ploughlands, a flock of herring gulls saw the splash, and swung round, wheeling with petulant cries.

11 *Mended Kelt*

The splash was also seen by a boy as he was walking hurriedly across the meadow, carrying rod in one hand and tailer in the other. At the sight he began to run. When near the bank, he bent down, and approached more slowly, lest his footfalls be felt by the fish.

Kneeling, and giving repeated glances at the tail of the run, he drew a box of Devon minnows from a pocket and selected one. It was a two-inch length of phosphor bronze, a dull yellow. This he threaded on a trace of thin steel wire set with swivels. At the extremity of the trace was a red bead above a triangle of hooks bound together. The minnow slipped down against the red bead. Then he drew line from the reel through the agate rings of his rod and tied it to the wire trace. The minnow dangled gleaming in the sun. One of the treble hook points touched the tweed cloth of his trousers, and instantly, although slight the touch, was fixed there by its barb. The minnow suggested the shape of a tiny fish, with pectoral fins that were a two-bladed screw. These, when the lure was drawn through the water, caused it to spin on the pivot of the read bead.

The rod was four feet long, made of steel, thinner than a rapier. It belonged to the boy's father, who had used it when fishing for black bass in rivers of Florida, which moved deep and dark under cedar trees hung with air-moss.

The reel also was American, small, simple, and level-winding. It ran smooth as oil, silently releasing plaited silk line through the rod rings while the lure dropped to the grass. The boy wound the minnow to the top of the rod, and screwed up the clutch until the minnow, weighing little more than an ounce, just ceased to pull line off the drum. The clutch would prevent back-lash of the line on the drum when casting.

Now everything was ready. He crept to the roots of an alder recently cut, found and tested foothold, stood upright cautiously, secured balance, gripped the rod in his right hand with thumb on bevelled side of reel drum and index finger crooked round the special hold, and then, with a sweep and jerk of the little rod as he had often seen his father do, sent the minnow three-quarter way across the river. As it fell with a slight splash he slowed the reel by pressing on the bevelled drum edge with his thumb, and, changing hands on the rod, began to wind in slowly, feeling the spinning drag of the lure under water. He quivered with excitement as a fish launched itself half out of the water behind the line, showing pointed dark grey head and white throat above its own wave.

It was Gralaks who had jumped; or rather, she had driven her body along the edge of the water to drag off the sea-lice from under her tail. They had ceased to feed, being sick in river water, and their unusual stillness was as an itch. The grilse had seen the lure, but had taken only the least notice of it, since a length of trace also had fallen into her cone of skylight.

The boy wound in the minnow, and tried to cast it in the same place, but it fell farther across the run, in front of Salar, who saw with his right eye a whir of light moving away in the water before him. Although it was moving centrally away from him, Salar did not see it with both eyes because his left eye was sun-dazed. It wobbled in the faster surface water, sometimes scattering behind it small bubbles. Salar had a desire to take it. He swam up and was turning under it with open mouth when something flashed hugely beside him and seized it.

As the kelt's bony jaws clashed on metal with sharp pain he opened his jaws to take in water and so to expel it; but it remained hard in his mouth. He could not close his jaws. He was not frightened, because in his past sea-life he had occasionally taken food which hurt his mouth by its hardness and gave pain by its poison when crushed. He turned down to the bed of the pool to find a stone against which to rub it off.

To the kelt's surprise and alarm, he could not get to the bed of the pool. He could not swim freely as hitherto in his life. He shook his head violently; the thing in his mouth stabbed him, and tugged at him strongly. A shock of fear jagged through his body, stimulating him to violent action. Desperately he shook his head again, and leapt quickly from the water three times without knowing what he was doing until it happened. The aerial scene was a tilted blur of blue and green and white. In his open gills the air was harsh and choking. When in water again he turned with the flow and swam away with all his strength, causing the hovering grilse to scatter and instantly to sink to the bottom. A fresh-run cock-fish of forty pounds' weight who had just moved up through the fast glide by the islet was so scared by an apparition rushing upon him with open jaws that he gave a jump and found himself unexpectedly in air and then falling on water on his back.

The terrified kelt turned in the rough water which had been pressing his gills open, and lay behind a boulder, curling his tail against a stone that was not there.

Eighty yards away on the bank the boy held the rod with both hands, one thumb pressed tightly against the drum, and wondered what he should do. He put a steady strain on the steel until his wrists were aching, and he feared the line would snap. It was of plaited silk, with a breaking strain of fifteen pounds. At last in fatigue he eased the strain on his trembling arms.

Behind the stone the kelt lay in distressed bewilderment. He could not understand this enemy that prevented him from breathing (for one barb of the triple hook was fixed in his tongue and a second barb in his vomer ridge or palate) and which held him although it never pursued him. Indeed the kelt did not yet define an enemy, although he was hiding in fear from the wire trace which extended taut in front of him, which vibrated its menace through his head and body.

He lay there, feeling weak and gulping jerkily, until the trace slackened, and feeling free, he moved sideways to rub his jaw against the edge of the stone. Since the trace did nothing to him his strength returned, and he swam hard against the stone, striking it with his head. The smolt and other food he had eaten were disgorged involuntarily in the struggle. The hooks drove deeper, and levered one against the other as he strove to wrench the thing from its hold in his mouth. The wounds, enlarged by the barbs, began to bleed. In pain and fury the kelt dashed the trace on the stone, with such force that the minnow was impelled up the trace, and the barb pierced the main artery of his body, which lay under the tongue.

As he bled he weakened. He began to swim up into the pool again, away from the slight drag of the water on the trace behind him; but when the pull came from before him he swung round again and in desperation of life swam down the river to the sea, imagined refuge.

He could not breathe, swimming downstream less fast than the stream. He had to turn, and in a frenzy of fear he swam back into the Junction Pool with jaggered strength and leapt to shake off the wounding hardness in his mouth. Falling back, he felt the water too strong for him, it swept him away, he lost sense and power of direction, his body heavy with fatigue. The drift rested him, and he recovered, to swim feebly the way he was being drawn, sometimes trying to swim aside, but in vain. He was exhausted. Drawn near the bank, into slower water, he saw his enemy, and the shock stimulated his wasted muscles. He struggled to reach the run, and in his effort to bore down into deeper water the river became strange and unfamiliar.

Exultingly the boy drew in the salmon to the bank, where it turned on its side, and lay still. Holding rod in one hand, with the other he passed the loop of the tailer over the fish's tail. It was like a short-handled whip with a loop of twisted steel wire for thong, and when lifted up with a jerk, the spring loop slid small, noosing the tail.

The kelt struggled as it was being lifted, it flapped feebly on the grass, but three blows of the priest on its head killed it. Its captor was trembling with pride and joy, and with these feelings was a slightness

Michael J. Loates.

of regret that it was no longer alive and free in the river. Later when he reached home the stannic lustre of the kelt was gone, its skin had shrunken, and its head looked too big for its body. To the boy's mortification, his father said it was a kelt. But, declared the boy, it was so bright that surely it was a clean-run fish, although there were no sea-lice on it. Then his father showed him the fresh-water maggots on the gill-rakers, a sure sign, he said: and for confirmation, there was the spawning mark on the point of balance by the paired fins—where scales and skin had been worn away by the act of digging gravel, he said. The mark, however, had not been caused by spawning (as such abrasions were generally regarded by anglers of the Two Rivers), but by prolonged resting on gravel or rock during the stagnancies of summer river life.

When cut the flesh was seen to be pale and infirm, and the carcase was buried under an apple tree in the orchard.

12 *Sloping Weir*

Clouds were slowly filling the air, paling the sun to a small white disc, gradually absorbing colours of sky and land until the afternoon was dull and cold. No fish showed in the Junction Pool. An angler with a double-handed rod of split cane sixteen feet long fished the water patiently, departing at sunset, which showed as a purple-grey heaviness down the valley.

The wind was from the north-west, piling up massive dark clouds which fell in cold hard rain upon the moors. Since the larger river, descending from the granite moor, lay below a main traffic road with its hundreds of lesser roads passing by hamlets and villages, it was soon turbid, and tainted with artificial fertilizers washed into its water; while the smaller river, passing undrained meadows and few houses on its way from the moor of the wild red deer, changed but slightly in colour and volume. By sunrise it had risen two inches, while the larger river was a foot higher. Fish moved farther up the pool, and to one side, lying in clearer water.

Later in the morning more fish moved into the Pool behind them, fresh-run from the top of the tide, and soon the salmon which had been resting there began to rise short, showing only the tops of heads and tails: slow, lackadaisical movements, as excitement or power began to spread through their bodies. When the water pressure began slightly to lessen, they set off, swimming slowly, as though leisurely, into the fast water of the new river, which swirled with air bubbles around its gravelly bed.

Had Salar and the larger fish been visible to a human eye, they would have appeared to be moving forward against rapid water while remaining immobile. Seldom would the sideway flexion of any fish have been apparent. Under a swift and broken stream a fish would be seen advancing as though the flow of water were without force. For while the surface streams of the river ran confused and fast, irregularly conforming to the rocky irregularities of the river-bed, the lower water was in reaction against the river-bed. Where it rushed fast on top, it might be almost still below, or even in reverse movement. In the river were innumerable weighted streams in competition for the force of gravity, delayed by friction in passage over obstructions of rocks, trees, pools, and banks. The salmon moved forward with casual ease in gaps and lanes of the streams' traffic, usually in delayed water.

At length Salar came to a bend in the river where on the edge of broken rapid water a circular pool was in motion. Many fish were waiting in the pool, which was caused to revolve by a great bubble-churning rush of white water surging down the face of a sloping weir. The sill of the weir had been built with a cut or nick in its centre for the passage of fish. Here, therefore, the water was most violent in its descent, flinging itself in white surges against the edge of the deeper water below, making it to turn.

The nearer edge of the water lapped a bank of shillets which had been dug out of the pool and left there by spates after the building of the weir. The bank of loose flat fragments of rock shelved deeply. Sometimes the tail-fin of a waiting fish showed a yard or less from the edge, to sink again casually. Nearer the pool's centre dorsal fins lifted above the ruffled surface. A heron flying overhead saw a blotch of dark blue in the water, where fish were massed.

Other eyes too were watching, from behind a hurdle of sticks and weeds left by the receding spate against the trunk of an alder tree on the bank a score of yards below the pool.

One of the fish resting there shook its tail and swam down slowly, rolling on its side and turning up again in another direction, cruising around the pool against the circular current. It was a fish which had been in the lower reaches of the river since the New Year. It was about to make its fourth attempt to ascend the weir. At three points on the rim of the pool it rolled out of the water, showing dorsal and tail fins as it gathered its will within itself; then, heading resolutely into the secondary rush of bubbled water alongside the white, it moved along the rocky bottom, and straightly swam up, accelerating with all its strength.

The winter salmon, flanks of tarnished silver and rust, leapt just beside, and clear of, the white thrust of water. It fell on the lower edge of the weir's apron, entering the thick cord of water descending from the gap in the sill above. The apron or face of the weir sloped at an angle of about 20°. Slowly the salmon, swimming with all its power, ascended the cord, and when half-way up its strength grew less and it ceased to advance: it stayed during the time of a double wing-beat of the heron wheeling overhead: desperately it turned aside in the hope of finding easier water, and was swept down on its side, tossed from wave to wave of the white surge to which it abandoned itself, and, reaching the end of the water's thrust, with a slow sweep of the tail entered the circular pool and took place among the other fish which had failed to get over the weir.

On the farther side of the weir stood a pine tree. The heron alighted on the topmost branch, and perched there swaying, holding its head up as anxiously it watched for its only enemy—man. The grassy bank below the tree ended in a masoned wall, under which the broken water surged over steps made to help fish over the obstruction of the weir. It was not known to the designer of the weir that a series of ledges, one below the other, would be avoided by salmon, although they had been built specially for them; the plan had seemed perfect. But running water usually does the opposite of what is expected of it by those not water-minded. The spate pouring over the sill down the steps made a white turbulence feared by every fish which ventured into it. There was no direct force of flow: it was water in rebound from stone and again in rebound from rebounding water: white shallow meaningless water which salmon dread. While the heron watched in the pine tree, Salar, after one preparatory roll, swam under the main stream and leapt tentatively, testing its force and direction. He was flung over backwards.

The scoop in the centre of the weir was made for the ease and safety of running fish, a spillway to enable them to ascend in moderate water. In the spates of early spring and late autumn, when salmon were running most numerously, the steps were impassable; and the central spine or flume was too strong. So salmon sought the easiest way, which was up the smooth slope of the weir rising from the inner bend of the pool below. This slope or apron was made of stone smoothed with concrete. The edge lay a few inches below the grassy slope of the meadow. Water ran thin at the edge, gradually deepening towards the central flume. The graduated weight of water falling made a diagonal line of white-bubbled surge across the pool, which thereby was one great revolving eddy. After exploring the major streams and finding them unswimmable, salmon either waited for less water or ventured to ascend at the point of least resistance, which was at the edge of the concrete slope, where it adjoined the sward of the meadow. Thus were they, in leaping, exposed to the danger to avoid which the weir was so designed: the gaffs of poachers.

Perched swaying in the pine top, the heron gazed around for human enemies; while behind the rough hurdle of sticks and leaves against an alder other eyes watched the heron, that unconscious sentinel for the men waiting there.

A bronze-coloured salmon, with black and green gill-covers and frayed tail-fin, jumped from deep water at the edge of the concrete slope and fell with a splash on its side, where it lay inert for a moment before the water washed it against the grass. It was half stunned, but the unfamiliar movement of water breaking over the nerves of its lateral line caused it to curve upright, steady itself with its pectoral fins, and with a wriggle to slip down the slope. As it did so, a string of yellowish pink eggs was washed away from it, into the pool below. This fish was a rawner, a female which had come in from the sea late, in the second week of December, and been unable to find a mate; nearly half its thirteen thousand eggs had been aimlessly shed. Some of those eggs, extruded by the shock of falling on the weir-face, were seized by a trout on the bed of the pool watching the edge of the bubble-turn, before the dark and gleaming shape of the rawner slid into and out of the trout's window of vision.

One of the men squatting behind the stick-heap was binding with string the shank of a gaff to a six-foot length of ash-plant which he had cut lower down by the river. The gaff was forged of iron, a large barbless hook. The shank was eight inches long, convenient size for concealing in the pocket.

The poachers were hiding because they had heard that one of the water-bailiffs was in the neighbourhood, having only that morning come upon two boys worming in the big junction pit below, without a salmon licence. After taking the boys' names and addresses, the bailiff had gone on up the valley, and might be about by the weir. They kept still, knowing that the heron's eye would detect the least movement. About half-past twelve, they reckoned, the bailies would be at their dinners, a good time to snatch a few fish, hide them in a sack until darkness, and away.

Up in the dark green branches, tipped with the brown of new growth, the heron flapped to shift position, and then looked around anxiously, lest the flapping might have attracted attention from its enemies. Like most of the herons fishing the valleys of the Two Rivers and their feeder streams, the bird had often heard a loud crack followed by the whistle and rattle of shot when surprised by man. Quite half the bird's working hours were passed in waiting and watching lest one of its enemies appear suddenly to surprise it.

When one of the men waiting below had whipped the gaff to the ash handle he took a small stone from a torn pocket of his coat and began to stroke the point to needle sharpness.

Down the side slope of the weir a kelt, with broken back-fin creamy with fungus disease, its back and sides also blotched, its head black and its underjaw prolonged in an upturned hook or kype, its body lean and brown, was washed, rolled over by the water it could no longer control. This fish had ascended the weir in its dashing Atlantic pride exactly a year before, a master of water which served its species and was servant to all fish only while they were strong with its running strength. Exhausted by disease below the point when it could mend itself by a spurt of its last stored strength, the fish was passing beyond the life-stream which flowed within the flow of the river. It had been resting above the weir since the night before, apprehensive of the water's roar below. Now the water turned it over and the scooping roll of bubbles took it into the pool, where it swayed into balance and rested, gulping water irregularly through its gills.

Salar lobbed himself half out of the water, feeling suddenly playful, and enjoying the nearness of many other fish like himself. Without real determination to ascend the weir, he swam strongly under the white thrust and up through it, appearing to the watching men to stand on his tail a moment before toppling backwards and disappearing.

The January-run fish tried again. It leapt from the deep water at the lower edge of the apron and splashed down on the slope, flapping sideways at the rate of nearly two hundred flaps a minute, appearing to plough its way upwards, a plume of water over its head. Making no progress, it altered direction and travelled aslant the glide, until it was within a foot of the edge of the grass, when it felt itself heavy with fatigue and ceased to swim, lying there, a crescent fish, a moment before turning its nose down and slipping back into the white churn several yards distant from where it had leapt.

Its long green toes gripping scaly boughs with excitement, and cursed in a low throaty monotone by a female carrion crow sitting on five eggs in her nest in a lower fork of the pine, the heron, giving a final hasty twist of its long neck as it glanced around, prepared to jump up and glide down to the side of the weir.

As the lanky grey bird paused, Trutta, big, black-spotted and dark stain of bruise three inches deep on his shoulders, lobbed himself vertically out beside the central white thrust and was swept over on

Michael J. Loates 1984

his back immediately. He knew by experience that the fall of water was too great. The old sea trout had swum over the weir more than a dozen times, and on the last half-dozen occasions he had swum up easily, although strenuously: always at night, and when the water was the right height. Trutta had jumped in lighter noon airs because the feeling of the many salmon in the pool was stimulating; and because the pain behind his head was lessening. His neck itched, and he was trying to knock the itching away against the water.

The sight of the large white belly and red of open gills made the heron launch itself from the tree and glide steeply down over the river, to alight with counter beat of wings on the grass above the sill of the weir. From this vantage point it waited, watching for movement of a hidden enemy. The heron was very old, and it knew that men with guns often hid by trees. Every time it came to this weir it spent several minutes in the top of the pine, and an equal period on the bank above the sill, before stalking slowly down to its fishing stance at the bottom of the water-slide.

Behind the screen of flood branches the man who had been sharpening the point of the gaff restrained his younger companion by a finger lift and part closing one eye.

Gralaks and the other grilse remaining from the shoal which had travelled together from the Island Race to the estuary were swimming under the cliff by which the surge from the weir swirled and swung before flowing as normal river again. Blue-grey heads and fins showed in the rocking surface. The grilse were in high glee with the boisterous water, parr-spirited but free of the selfish concentration of their parr-hood. One of the hiding men stared, because the tail-fin of one fish looked black, and sharply forked, more like a mackerel's tail than a salmon's. It had been snapped at by a porpoise, which had bitten away the centre of its tail-fin. These grilse curving out of the surge had a greenish tinge above the medial line: finishing diet of sprats off the south-west coast of Ireland. "Greenbacks," muttered the elder of the two men, "rinned up late." Greenbacks usually arrived in early winter.

The heron stood on the bank above the top of the weir, where the water from the pool was led away in the leat to the grist-mill a quarter of a mile distant. On the tree-top his suspicions of possible enemies had slowly been stared away; now a different aspect upon the landscape recreated them once more. The heron swayed its head in the hope of being able to look round the trunks of trees. It searched the path across the river, above the small cliff under which the river surged, and the top of the vegetable garden wall beyond. It had seen a man working in the garden while flying over, but as he was always there and had never shown notice, the heron looked away after the least glance.

A fish splashed into the white skirts of the weir, and was kicked back immediately. The heron started to walk down the grassy slope, but hesitated in alarm that its field of vision was diminishing with every step; it paused and lifted up its head and looked around. It saw the miller, a familiar figure, come out of the mill-house a quarter of a mile away, and with a bar lever up the fender by the wheel, for the sluice to run away during the dinner hour. The wheel had already stopped turning; it was one o'clock. The heron also saw another man walking down the road. This was the water-bailiff, who had been inquiring of the miller if he had seen any fish under his mill-wheel.

The miller's stag-bird, a gamecock living arrogantly among various hens, shook its wet wings on the bank of the water-course below. The opening of the fender had sent water sluicing down in a wave, and the bird, walking in the thin stickle of water and hunting small fish, had been swept off its feet. This did not bother the gamecock, which often before had been soused like this. Whenever it saw the fender being closed this bird ran to the bank and entered the stream as the flow was sinking and struck with its beak at any trout it saw reaming in shallow water. The bird was a clumsy and miniature heron; but it had a measure of skill, and when in summer and early autumn the small sea-trout, called peal, were running, and the fender was closed, it ran with flapping wings to the stream-side, to take the spotted mother-of-pearl fish and open them on the bank for the orange-pink eggs within, its favourite food. The miller was an honest man, and never took a salmon from the pit below the sluice; and he told the water-bailiff, with equal honesty as he went to dinner, unrolling shirt sleeves over thick forearms, that never yet had he seen any poacher take salmon or peal from his mill-stream. As the water-bailiff walked away, the cock crowed, and then proceeded to inspect its hens while waiting for the fender to close again at two o'clock.

Its hunger at last overcoming anxiety, the heron stalked stiltedly down the grassy slope and stepped on the edge of the concrete at the base of the sill, by a crack where a dock root and a thistle root were about to unfurl their first leaves of the year. It assured itself of a good hold for its long green feet and peered over the water, holding beak down to strike should any sizeable fish appear. Then it gave a jump and uttered a skwark and beat up violently, seeing two men rising out of the gravel bank near it. With long legs trailing, it flapped down the river, swerving as it saw the figure of a man looking over the road bridge.

This was the water-bailiff who wondered what had disturbed the heron, for he knew it had been startled by the quick way it had been beating its wings when it had first come into view. The weir was hidden by a bend and trees from the bridge. He decided to go to the weir.

Crouching by the edge where the heron had been standing, the man with the gaff waited for a fish to show. His mate kept a look out on the bank above.

A salmon, which had not seen the men, suddenly leapt in panic from the far edge of the pool and as it did so the poacher saw something thin fall from its head.

The poacher was waiting, as still as a heron but not so well clad, gaff in hand ready to snatch the first fish to come within reach, staring at the water, when his mate turned casually towards him and shouted out "Bailie!" while pretending to crouch from an imaginary wind in order to light a cigarette. Without turning his head or shifting his position, but with an instant movement of the lower parts of his arms, the poacher lanced the gaff into the white strakes of the surge. It turned up in the water before disappearing. Putting hands in pockets of torn jacket, the man stood there looking at the water until, a couple of minutes later, he turned his head slowly to the voice of the Bailie saying, "Ha, caught you this time, have I, Shiner?"

The poacher, known as Shiner for his work during moonlit nights, replied, "Have 'ee got a fag in your pocket, midear?" "Aiy," said the bailiff. "And have 'ee got a gaff in yours, by any chance, Shiner?"

"Aw, I ban't no water-whipping rod-and-line gentry, you should know that, midear. What be the like o' me wanting a gaff for? You'll be asking me for a gennulman's licence next, or the loan of a maskell's guts and kid's coloured fishing fly. Search me if it will plaize 'ee, midear."

A maskell was the local name for caterpillar, and the old fellow's reference, which the slower-witted bailiff did not understand, was to silkworm gut.

"You know I ban't allowed by law to search you," retorted the water-bailiff, disconcerted by the poacher's good humour. "Got a gaff hidden under they bushes, have 'ee?"

"I ban't stopping you from searching, midear."

"Well, then, will 'ee answer why you'm waiting yurr?"

"Elvers be running, midear. They'm poaching your fish, too, I fancy. Why don't 'ee summon they elvers, midear?"

He pointed to the water turning back under the bank, where a diseased and dying kelt had turned up slowly on its side, a dark mass of midget eels wriggling round it. Its gills were clustered with wriggles. The fish swam away slowly, doomed to be eaten alive.

"There ban't no law against a poor man taking a dish of elvers for his tea, be there?" inquired Shiner, as he took off a weather-stained felt hat. He knelt down and dipped it in the water. A dozen elvers swam around inside. He threw them back, and banged the hat on the grass to knock off the water. "Well, midear, us mustn't keep th' ould crane from his dinner, must us? Else they Cruelty to Hanimals people will be after us, won't n?"

Shiner pointed to the heron passing over high, flying slowly, legs straight out behind and neck tucked in. He walked away, laughing loudly.

13 Black Dog

The elvers were running. They darkened the green shallows of the river. The eddies were thick tangles of them. They had come into the estuary on the flood-tide, and in a gelatinous mass had moved into the still water of the tide-head. All fish in the river sped from them, for elvers were gill-twisting torture and death.

For nearly three years as thin glassy threads the young eels had been crossing the Atlantic, drifting in warm currents of the Gulf Stream from the Sargasso Sea. Here in deep water far under floating beds of clotted marine wreckage, all the mature eels of the northern hemisphere, patient travellers from inland ponds and ditches, brooks and rivers, came together to shed themselves of life for immortal reasons. From blue dusk of ocean's depth they passed into death: and from darkness the elvers arose again, to girdle the waters of half the earth.

Salar lay in fast water between Sloping Weir and the road bridge. He lay in front of a large stone, in the swift flume rising to pass over it. The flume streamed by his head and gills and shoulders without local eddy. No elver could reach his gill without violent wriggling, which he would feel. He was swift with the swiftness of the water. There was the least friction between fish and river, for his skin exuded a mucus or lubricant by which the water slipped. The sweep of strong water guarded his life. Other salmon were lying in like lodges in the stony surges. Salar lodged there until dusk, when he moved forward again. Gralaks moved beside him. They recognized and knew each other without greeting.

Many fish were at Sloping Weir now, waiting beside the lessening weight of white water, in the swarming bubbles of the eddy. They lay close to one another. As soon as one fish waggled tail and dipped and rose to get a grip of the water, to test its own pulse of power, another fish took its place, ready for the take-off. Salar idled, alert, apprehensive, seventeenth in line. Sometimes two or three fish left the phalanx at the same time and after nervous ranging set themselves to swim up through the heavy water looking like snow under the rising moon.

At the edge of the turning pool, where the poachers had waited and watched during the day, stood Shiner's "ould Crane". The bird was picking up elvers as fast as he could snick them. His throat and neck ached. A continuous loose rope of elvers wove itself on the very edge of the water, where frillets sliding down the concrete apron-edge washed elvers into the grass.

After a return to the tree-top heronry where three hernlets had craked and fought to thrust their beaks down his throat to take what he had, Old Nog flew back to the weir and picked and swallowed slowly, his excitement gone, for the elvers were not for him. He flew home again, and by the light of the full moon returned with his mate to the weir. They crammed their crops and necks and flew back to their filthy nest, where by midnight the three hernlets were crouching, huddled and dour with overmuch feeding. Old Nog then flew back to the weir, to feed himself. Most of the elvers were by then gone, but he managed, for the moment, to satisfy his hunger.

On the way home, however, an elver wriggled down his windpipe, causing him to choke and sputter and disgorge; the mass fell beside a badger below rubbing against its scratching-thorn, causing it to start and grunt with alarm. Having cautiously sniffed for some minutes, from various angles, the badger dared to taste; after which it ate all up and searched for more. For the next few nights it returned specially to rub itself against the thorn, in the hope of finding such food there again. As for Old Nog, not an elver that year reached his long pot, as countrymen do call the guts.

During the time of the moon's high tides, more than two hundred salmon passed over the weir. Salar swam up on his second attempt; at first he had been unsure of himself, and dropped back almost as soon as he had got a grip on the central cord or spine of water. Swimming again with all his power, he moved slowly into the glissade of water above the white surge, stayed a third of the way up, as though motionless, vibrating; then had gained over the water and swum stronger in jubilation, and suddenly found the sill moving away under him, release of weight from his sides, and calm deep water before him. He flung himself out for joy, and a young dog-otter, which was rolling on its back on grass at the pool's edge, where a bitch-otter had touched earlier in the night, instantly lifted its head, slipped to the edge, put its head under, and slid tail last into the water.

Salar saw the otter swimming above him, shining in a broken envelope of air on head and fur and legs. The pool took the dull blows of his acceleration and in three seconds, when the otter had swum nine yards against the current, Salar had gone twenty yards upstream into the mill-pool, swerved from a sunken tree trunk lodged in the silt, zigzagged forward to the farther bank, startling other salmon resting there, and hidden himself under a ledge of rock. The otter, which was not hunting salmon, since in deep water it could never catch any, unless a fish were injured, crawled out on the bank again to enjoy through its nose what it imagined visually.

An elver wriggled against Salar, and he swam on. The pool was long and deep and dark. He swam on easily, restfully, slower than the pace of the otter's pretended chase. The wound in his side began to ache dully, and he rested near the surface, near water noisy over a branch of alder. At dawn he was three miles above Sloping Weir, lying under a ledge of rock hollow curving above him, and therefore protecting him from behind, with an immediate way of escape from danger into deep water. The salmon slept, only the white-grey tip of the kype—hooked end of lower jaw—showing as the mouth slightly opened. Fifteen times a minute water passed the gills, which opened imperceptibly.

Salar slept. The water lightened with sunrise. He lay in shadow. His eyes were fixed, passively susceptible to all movement. The sun rose up. Leaves and stalks of loose weed and water-moss passing were seen but unnoticed by the automatic stimulus of each eye's retina. The eyes worked together with the unconscious brain, while the nerves, centres of direct feeling, rested themselves. One eye noticed a trout hovering in the water above, but Salar did not see it.

The sun rose higher, and shone down on the river, and slowly the shadow of the ledge shrank into its base. Light revealed Salar, a grey-green uncertain dimness behind a small pale spot appearing and disappearing regularly.

Down there Salar's right eye was filled with the sun's blazing fog. His left eye saw the wall of rock and the water above. The trout right forward of him swam up, inspected that which had attracted it, and swam down again; but Salar's eye perceived no movement. The shadow of the trout in movement did not fall on the salmon's right eye.

A few moments later there was a slight splash left forward of Salar. Something swung over, casting the thinnest shadow; but it was seen by the eye, which awakened the conscious brain. Salar was immediately alert.

The thing vanished. A few moments later, it appeared nearer to him.

With his left eye Salar watched the thing moving overhead. It swam in small jerks, across the current and just under the surface, opening and shutting, gleaming, glinting, something trying to get away. Salar, curious and alert, watched it until it was disappearing and then he swam up and around to take it ahead of its arc of movement. The surface water, however, was flowing faster than the river at mid-stream, and he misjudged the opening of his mouth, and the thing, which recalled sea-feeding, escaped.

On the bank upriver fifteen yards away a fisherman with fourteen-foot split-cane rod said to himself, excitedly, "Rising short"; and pulling loops of line between reel and lowest ring of rod, he took a small pair of scissors from a pocket and snipped off the thing which had attracted Salar.

No wonder Salar had felt curious about it, for human thought had ranged the entire world to imagine that lure. It was called a fly; but no fly like it ever swam in air or flew through water. Its tag, which had glinted, was of silver from Nevada and silk of a moth from Formosa; its tail, from the feather of an Indian crow; its butt, black herl of African ostrich; its body, yellow floss-silk veiled with orange breast-feathers of the South American toucan, and black Macclesfield silk ribbed with silver tinsel. This fly was given the additional attraction of wings for water-flight, made of strips of feathers from many birds: turkey from Canada, peahen and peacock from Japan, swan from Ireland, bustard from Arabia, golden-pheasant from China, teal and wild duck and mallard from the Hebrides. Its throat was made of the feather of an English speckled hen, its side of Bengal jungle-cock's neck feathers, its cheeks came from a French kingfisher, its horns from the tail of an Amazonian macaw. Wax, varnish, and enamel secured the "marriage" of the feathers. It was one of hundreds of charms, or materialized river-side incantations, made by men to persuade sleepy or depressed salmon to rise and take. Invented after a bout of seasickness by a Celt as he sailed the German Ocean between England and Norway, for nearly a hundred years this fly had borne his name, Jock Scott.

While the fisherman was tying a smaller pattern of the same fly to the end of the gut cast, dark stained by nitrate of silver against under-water glint, Salar rose to mid-water and hovered there. Behind him lay the trout, which, scared by the sudden flash of the big fish turning, had dropped back a yard. So Salar had hovered three years before in his native river, when, as parr spotted like a trout, and later as silvery smolt descending to the sea, he had fed eagerly on nymphs of the olive dun and other ephemeridae coming down with the current.

He opened his mouth and sucked in a nymph as it was swimming to the surface. The fisherman saw a swirl on the water, and threw his fly, with swish of double-handed rod, above and to the right of the swirl. Then, lowering the rod point until it was almost parallel to the water, he let the current take the fly slowly across the stream, lifting the rod tip and lowering it slightly and regularly to make it appear to be swimming.

Salar saw the fly and slowly swam up to look at it. He saw it clear in the bright water and sank away again, uninterested in the lifelessness of its bright colours. Again it reappeared, well within his skylight window. He ignored it, and it moved out of sight. Then it fell directly over him, jigging about in the water, and with it a dark thin thing which he regarded cautiously. This was the gut cast. Once more it passed over, and then again, but he saw only the dark thinness moving there. It was harmless. He ignored it. Two other salmon below Salar, one in a cleft of rock and the other beside a sodden oak log wedged under the bank, also saw the too-bright thing, and found no vital interest in it.

The fisherman pulled in the line through the rod-rings. It was of plaited silk, tapered and enamelled for ease of casting. The line fell over his boot. Standing still, he cut off the fly and began a search for another in a metal box, wherein scores of mixed feathers were ranged on rows of metal clasps. First he moved one with his forefinger, then another, staring at this one and frowning at that one, recalling in its connection past occasions of comparative temperatures of air and river, of height and clearness of water, of sun and shade, while the angler's familiar feeling, of obscurity mingled with hope and frustration, came over him. While from the air he tried to conjure certainty for a choice of fly, Salar, who had taken several nymphs of the olive dun during the time the angler had been cogitating, leapt and fell back with a splash that made the old fellow take a small Black Doctor and tie the gut to the loop of the steel hook with a single Cairnton jam-knot.

Salar saw this lure and fixed one eye on it as it approached and then ignored it, a thing without life. As it was being withdrawn from the water a smolt which had seen it only then leapt open-mouthed at a sudden glint and fell back, having missed it.

Many times a similar sort of thing moved over Salar, who no longer heeded their passing. He enjoyed crushing the tiny nymphs on his tongue, and tasting their flavour. Salar was not feeding, he was not hungry; but he was enjoying remembrance of his river-life with awareness of an unknown great excitement before him. He was living by the spirit of running water. Indeed Salar's life was now the river: as he explored it higher, so would he discover his life.

On the bank the fisherman sat down and perplexedly re-examined his rows and rows of flies. He had tried all recommended for the water, and several others as well; and after one short rise, no fish had come to the fly. Mar Lodge and Silver Grey, Dankeld and Black Fairy, Beauly Snow Fly, Fiery Brown, Silver Wilkinson, Thunder and Lightning, Butcher, Green Highlander, Blue Charm, Candlestick Maker, Bumbee, Little Inky Boy, all were no good. Then in one corner of the case he saw an old fly of which most of the mixed plumage was gone: a Black Dog which had belonged to his grandfather. Grubs of moths had fretted away hackle, wing, and topping. It was thin and bedraggled. Feeling that it did not matter much what fly was used, he sharpened the point with a slip of stone, tied it on, and carelessly flipped it into the water. He was no longer fishing; he was no longer intent, he was about to go home; the cast did not fall straight, but crooked; the line also was crooked. Without splash the fly moved down a little less fast than the current, coming thus into Salar's skylight. It was like the nymphs he had been taking, only larger; and with a leisurely sweep he rose and turned across the current, and took it, holding it between tongue and vomer as he went down to his lie again, where he would crush and taste it. The sudden resistance of the line to his movement caused the point of the hook to prick the corner of his mouth. He shook his head to rid himself of it, and this action drove the point into the gristle, as far as the barb.

A moment later, the fisherman, feeling a weight on the line, lifted the rod-point, and tightened the line, and had hardly thought to himself, *salmon*, when the blue-grey tail of a fish broke half out of water and its descending weight bended the rod.

Salar knew of neither fisherman nor rod nor line. He swam down to the ledge of rock and tried to rub the painful thing in the corner of his mouth against it. But his head was pulled away from the rock. He saw the line, and was fearful of it. He bored down to his lodge at the base of the rock, to get away from the line, while the small brown trout swam behind his tail, curious to know what was happening.

Salar could not reach his lodge. He shook his head violently, and, failing to get free, turned downstream and swam away strongly, pursued by the line and a curious buzzing vibration just outside his jaw.

Below the pool the shallow water jabbled before surging in broken white crests over a succession of rocky ledges. Salar had gone about sixty yards from his lodge, swimming hard against the backward pull of line, when the pull slackened, and he turned head to current, and lay close to a stone, to hide from his enemy.

When the salmon had almost reached the jabble, the fisherman, fearing it would break away in the rough water, had started to run down the bank, pulling line from the reel as he did so. By thus releasing direct pull on the fish, he had turned it. Then, by letting the current drag line in a loop below it, he made Salar believe that the enemy was behind him. Feeling the small pull of the line from behind, Salar swam up into deeper water, to get away from it. The fisherman was now behind the salmon, in a position to make it tire itself by swimming upstream against the current.

Salar, returning to his lodge, saw it occupied by another fish, which his rush, and the humming line cutting the water, had disturbed from the lie by the sodden log. This was Gralaks the grilse. Again Salar tried to rub the thing against the rock, again the pull, sideways and upwards, was too strong for him. He swam downwards, but could make no progress towards the rock. This terrified him and he turned upwards and swam with all his strength, to shake it from his mouth. He leapt clear of the water and fell back on his side, still shaking his head.

On the top of the leap the fisherman had lowered his rod, lest the fly be torn away as the salmon struck the water.

Unable to get free by leaping, Salar sank down again and settled himself to swim away from the enemy. Drawing the line after him, and beset again by the buzzing vibration, he travelled a hundred yards to the throat of the pool, where water quickened over gravel. He lay in the riffle spreading away from a large stone, making himself heavy, his swim-bladder shrunken, trying to press himself into the gravel which was his first hiding place in life. The backward pull on his head nearly lifted him into the fast water, but he held himself down, for nearly five minutes, until his body ached and he weakened and he found himself being taken down sideways by the force of shallow water. He recalled the sunken tree and it became a refuge, and he swam down fast, and the pull ceased with the buzz against his jaw. Feeling relief, he swam less fast over his lodge, from which Gralaks sped away, alarmed by the line following Salar.

But before he could reach the tree the weight was pulling him back, and he turned and bored down to bottom, scattering a drove of little grey shadows which were startled trout. Again the pull was too much for him, and he felt the ache of his body spreading back to his tail. He tried to turn on his side to rub the corner of his mouth on something lying on the bed of the pool—an old cartwheel—again and again, but he could not reach it.

A jackdaw flying silent over the river, paper in beak for nest-lining, saw the dull yellow flashes and flew faster in alarm of them and the man with the long curving danger.

Fatigued and aching, Salar turned downstream once more, to swim away with the river, to escape the enemy which seemed so

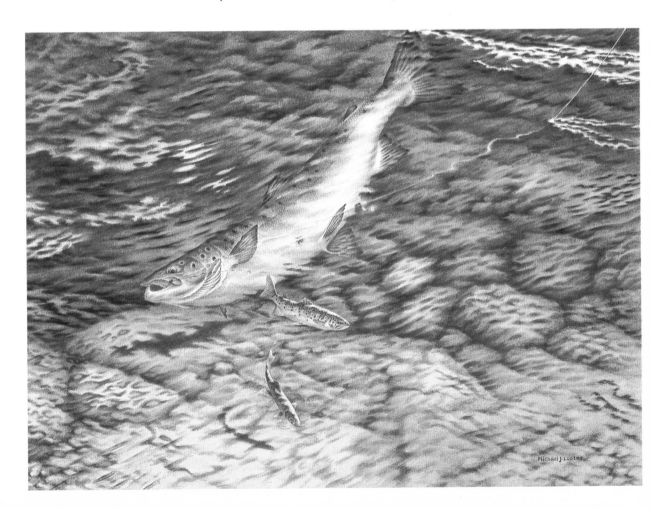

much bigger because he could not close his mouth. As he grew heavier, slower, uncertain, he desired above all to be in the deeps of the sea, to lie on ribbed sand and rest and rest and rest. He came to rough water, and let it take him down, too tired to swim. He bumped into a rock, and was carried by the current around it, on his side, while the gut cast, tautened by the dragging weight, twanged and jerked his head upstream, and he breathed again, gulping water quickly and irregularly. Still the pull was trying to take him forward, so with a renewal by fear he turned and re-entered fast water and went down and down, until he was in another deep pool at a bend of the river. Here he remembered a hole under the roots of a tree, and tried to hide there, but had not strength enough to reach the refuge of darkness.

Again he felt release, and swam forward slowly, seeking the

deepest part of the pool, to lie on the bottom with his mouth open. Then he was on his side, dazed and weary, and the broken-quicksilvery surface of the pool was becoming whiter. He tried to swim away, but the water was too thick-heavy; and after a dozen sinuations it became solid. His head was out of water. A shock passed through him as he tried to breathe. He lay there, held by line taut over fisherman's shoulder. He felt himself being drawn along just under the surface, and only then did he see his enemy—flattened, tremulant-spreading image of the fisherman. A new power of fear broke in the darkness of his lost self. When it saw the tailer coming down to it, the surface of the water was lashed by the desperately scattered self. The weight of the body falling over backwards struck the taut line; the tail-fin was split. The gut broke just above the hook, where it had been frayed on the rock. Salar saw himself sinking down into the pool, and he lay there, scattered about himself and unable to move away, his tail curved round a stone, feeling only a distorted head joined to the immovable river-bed.

14 Denzil's Pool

All day Salar lay dull in the pool, under the roots of an alder, never moving. After the sun had set and other salmon were leaving their lies and lodges, he swam forward slowly, painfully. The wind had veered to the north-west, bringing hard-edged clouds towering in blackness above the moor. Down in the estuary at midnight fishermen hauled on nets which held, draught after draught, only seaweed and crabs; they said nothing at all, they had been wet in empty sea-labour most of their lives. Salmon from the sea jumped in the wide spate-water of the fairway and passed up one or other of the Two Rivers. Some of them, fast travellers, moved beside Salar when next evening's sun was spreading rubicund on the hill tops.

Salar followed these new keen fish, his weariness eased, and by sunrise was lying with them in a pool called Denzil's, wide and deep, above another grist-mill weir and the joining place of a third river. In this pool, which was deep because a ledge of rock crossed the river-bed, the clay below having been scooped out by the centuries' spates, lay thirty salmon.

Many of these fish moved on at nightfall, and new fish came in, with Trutta the sea-trout, but Salar remained there. He was apprehensive, and deep water gave serenity. Many times he turned on his side and tried to rub off the iron lacerating the corner of his mouth. Soon most of the skin was rubbed off his jawbone. Body movement was no longer painful, but all his muscles ached.

After a week had passed, the alder leaves growing on the banks above Denzil's Pool were large as the ears of mice which at night moved among the drying litter of twigs, marking the height of the spate on the bank above. One evening a field-mouse fell into the water, and was swimming to the bank when there was a plop, a black scarred neb showing, a jaw opening to reveal many teeth, a swirl on the empty surface. Garroo the cannibal trout had his home under the alder roots.

Atlantic rains falling on the moors had filled the springs in the rock, and the river kept its level for another week. Then it ran slower, and salmon in the middle and lower reaches of the Two Rivers settled down in their lies and lodges.

Every day Salar, resting at the edge of the deepening water, saw lines and lures, which he now recognized as enemies, moving, flickering, spinning at varying speeds over him. For a week the wind continued from the north-west, and nymphs delayed their hatching; and no salmon were taken from the pool, except one foul-hooked by a spinner which caught it in the gill, causing it to bleed to exhaustion in the water.

Salar had been waiting there nearly a fortnight when towards the end of a night, as the hollow ruin of the moon was rising through trees, two fish sped past him, turned in shelving water, and sank beside him. All the fish shared an alertness of fear. A light darted in the water, moved about, and went out. Another light shone behind them. Salar swam into the deepest water, where he could see most— forward, above, and behind. Fish swung and thudded about in alarm. A strange smell came to him in the water, and he accelerated to the farther side of the pool.

Two men were wading above the pool, on the edge of the transverse reef. They carried armfuls of net, which they let down into deep water. A third man held the end of the rope under the bank. Sixty yards away two other men were taking a trammel across the river, in shallowing water below the pool. A sixth man stood on the bank, waiting silent and listening in the last darkness of night. A heap of old potato sacks lay near him, the temporary bed of a lean hairy dog with long thin legs, head, and tail. This was a lurcher, shivering, curled as though to sleep, but flair-nosed, wide-eyed, cock-eared. It never barked or growled. It knew the smell of every water-bailiff in the catchment area of the Two Rivers. The dog and its master shared a soundless language, of attitude, glance, and movement.

Across the stickle, where lay the gravel scooped out of the pool, other men were fixing the trammel, consisting of two lengths of net, the outer of small mesh for holding, the inner of large loose squares for entangling, fish.

The six men belonged to a gang which worked pools of the Two Rivers only at night. The leader, who owned dog and nets, was a mild-mannered, bespectacled cabinet-maker by day. The lenses of his spectacles were of plain glass: he wore them to protect his eyes from wood-dust, and also, by their absence at night, as a disguise. Four of

Michael J. Coates

the men had been fined by the magistrates of the local town, for poaching. The fining had occurred before they had formed themselves into a gang, under the leadership of the cabinet-maker, since when none had been caught. Its members blackened their faces before leaving the old and unlicensed saloon car in which they travelled on their planned raids. One man, however, knew why the car was used only at night; and that man was Shiner.

Shiner had made and owned and used the trammel net, until he had been surprised one night by the bailiffs, who had confiscated it. Shiner had been summoned, convicted, sentenced to imprisonment; and the Court made an order for the destruction of the trammel net which had been produced as evidence against him. The trammel, however, had been stolen from the court room, during the second prosecution by the clerk to the Board of Conservators—a retired rear-admiral taking salmon with a trout licence only, the excuse being loss of memory due to the war.

The trammel net was never missed, because the local police authorities thought the water-bailiffs had carried it away, and the bailiffs thought the police had removed it. When he had served ten days in prison, Shiner, who had watched the net being taken, said nothing, although he knew who had it. He disliked the gang, because they sometimes worked with methods he considered dirty—they poisoned whole stretches of river by the use of chloride of lime, and blew the pits with gelignite, which destroyed all life in them. Shiner was awaiting an opportunity to get his own back in his own way; for he was not the sort of man to write anonymous letters to police or river-owner.

The gang did not know, when they left their car behind a haystack in a field by the road a quarter of a mile away, that Shiner was watching in the next field. His tool-cart—he was an odd-day gardener to various houses—was hidden behind another haystack. When the gang had left for the river, Shiner climbed through the hedge and, opening the bonnet of their car, unscrewed all the leads to the sparking plugs, fixing them again in wrong order; and then, to make sure the engine would not start, he emptied a small bag of sugar into the petrol tank. After this, struck by a sudden thought, he climbed through the hedge again and removed his tool-cart to the other end of the field, concealing it in a dip of the ground.

Some minutes later he crossed the lane and listened. Then he wetted a forefinger to reassure himself that the breeze was moving from Denzil's Pool in his direction. Afterwards he hid behind an oak tree on the bank above, and waited.

While he was standing there the drift net was spread across the river. Its lead-weighted heel-rope sank into deep water, its line of corks was bellied out by the surface current. Two men, one under each bank and holding an end of rope, began to work their way down the sides of the pool, wading sometimes to their armpits, and gripping branches which overhung the water.

As the drift net slowly moved upon them the salmon became agitated, and moved at great speed up and down the pool. One shot through the wide netting of the trammel, turned immediately from the close netting beyond, and was caught by the gills. The poachers heard the threshing of broken water, and began to work faster with the drift net. "Go easy," said the leader, standing on the bank above, a dim silhouette against the resolving twilight of dawn. Another fish began to splash.

In the centre of the pool lay Trutta, and near him were Salar and Gralaks. Trutta had known netting in Denzil's Pool two years before. Now, as the drift net came down, he swam aside to the alder, the roots of which in water were like many crayfish huddled together, and pushed under them. Because they recognized Trutta in the stimulation of fear which started old actions in memory, when they had followed him before and so escaped from a like danger, both Salar and Gralaks followed him now and thrust themselves under the mat of alder roots. They stayed there even when the noise and movement of legs was very near. As the disturbance went away another fish pushed in between Salar and Trutta, a terrified brown trout with a black and irregular under-jaw, immense head, sharp teeth, and lean body. This was Garroo the cannibal trout, who was fifteen years old, and weighed seven pounds, and who had long forgotten the fevers of spawning, but not the taste of trout and salmon eggs. In a fury of fear at finding his retreat occupied Garroo bit the tail of Gralaks, and received a slap on the side of his black horny head that caused him to lie limply, for several minutes, diagonally across the parallel bodies of Trutta and Salar.

While the four fish were hidden under the root-clump, the drift net was approaching the trammel. "Go easy," said the leader. The area between the two nets was slashed with gleams as fish turned and returned. Up to their middle in water, the men who had dragged the drift net were now hauling in the twin ropes of heel and head, only a few yards away from the trammel. The net-ends met on shelving gravel. Gradually the other end of the trammel was brought over, outside the drift net. Within the rocking corks more than a dozen salmon were struggling, torn of gill and tail, scales scraped off skin. The mass of fish was dragged to where the bank was broken by drinking cattle, and one by one they were hauled out on a gaff, and beaten on the nose by the cabinet-maker with a short club of yew-wood weighted with an inlaid spiral of brass.

Nine fish were laid out on the grass, the largest twenty-eight pounds, the smallest seven pounds—one of the grilse of the school led by Gralaks. Quickly nets were stowed into sacks, and the gang, jubilant and now smoking fags, set off across the fields to the lane. It was half an hour to dawn, the shine was already gone from the moon in the great azure glow spreading up the eastern sky. Clouds, hedges, haystacks to the west were black. Their feet rustled frosty grasses. Bullocks which had been crowding and snuffling, black-massed, into the corner by the gate, cantered away, ignored by the lurcher dog, which lifted one ear and glanced at its master, as a cock in the farmyard half a mile away crowed to the morning star.

For nearly an hour they tried to get the car started. First one, then another swung the handle, falling away and cursing in exhaustion.

The cabinet-maker took down the carburettor, and saw a dark sticky liquid, like crude petroleum, in the float chamber. Peering in the tank with the aid of an electric torch, he saw more of it lying at the bottom. He was bitter and blasphemous. It was run off; carburettor reassembled; handle swung again, many times, desperately. The eastern hill-line was a haze of shining, soon the sun would rise and labourers be about. They began to quarrel. Some wanted to divide the fish, and make off homewards across the fields: others, supporting the leader, argued that bestways they should be hid in the stack, and fetched at night. At last the others agreed; but one said, wouldn't the car give away the hiding place? So the salmon, wrapped in sacks, were carried to the adjoining haystack, which had been cut down one side, and concealed on the loose top of it. The nets were hidden in the hedge some distance away, and then, having washed the black from their faces in the ditch, the gang separated and went home across the fields.

A couple of hours later Shiner was wheeling his tool-cart, apparently laden with horse dung, across the market square of the small town. "Do you reckon it be time to till early tetties, midear?" he asked the police sergeant, who every year won prizes for potatoes in the local flower show. "Wait until the ground's in temper; 'tis no use mucketting," replied the sergeant, with amiable importance.

"You'm right," said Shiner, promptly. With a grin he added, "You'd like what I've got in this cart, I dare say? 'Tes proper stuff for growing big tetties."

The sergeant, who had had a kind thought for Shiner since he had been in prison for merely taking salmon, replied, "You keep it for yourself, Shiner; you worked hard enough for it, I reckon."

"You'm right, midear," agreed Shiner, as he went on his way.

That night many of the leading citizens of the town, including several magistrates, dined on salmon which had been bought, surreptiously, at their kitchen doors.

The old car was abandoned, and the gang broke up.

BOOK THREE

Book Three: Summer River

15 Sisters

By the edge of the shallow water two sand-pipers were walking, little brown-mottled birds, with long beaks and gentle eyes; meditative waterside birds, who had just flown from Abyssinia to their summer home by the stream. They were still in a dream of migration, their eyes saw the river and green meadows and great oaks and chestnuts on the hillside; but those eyes were sea-dazed, they were tired, they were content to be together by the edge of the grass and gravel, to hear the low song of water, to take a stone-fly just hatched from its larval skin on a dry stone, to see the white clouds in the blue above.

The sand-pipers had crossed the sea, arriving at the Island at dusk, resting there all night, and in the morning had flown to the estuary, and up the valley, following the river as it grew smaller and ran quicker, as it tumbled white between rocks and ran clear over stretches of yellow gravel.

A few miles away, on high ground under the northern sky, the river began its life in the rushes and cotton-grass bogs of the moor. Thither the minds of the sand-pipers were set, as they walked by the waterside, feeding lightly; sometimes rising scarcely higher than the level of the stream to fly a few yards, tremulously, as though flight for them now were a short trilling song of the gentle English spring.

Here the stream ran through a park, where fallow-deer roamed of olden time; now it was pasture for bullocks, black sheep, and horses. The horses were tall and powerful, muscles rippling under glossy skin, long tails swishing as they drank at the ford above the bridge. They were out to grass after the fox-hunting season. They drank slowly, sucking long and delicately, pawing the gravel, content in one another and the windy warmth of the April sun.

Half a dozen striding plunges took the leading horse, a black gelding called Midnight, across the river. The other horses followed, the water of the ford torn by their knees. They climbed out on the opposite bank, whinnying, as though teasing or challenging one another, red-nostrilled, bright-eyed, and suddenly they were galloping away, tails streaming from brown and grey and black. The sandpipers arose at the thud of hooves and flew on a few yards with tremulous slowness, before sinking again and walking gravely at the water verge.

Salar felt the thuds of hooves as the herd was crossing the ford. He was lying in deeper water twenty yards below, where the run slowed and glided uneven above the uneven stony bottom. Alders hung over the water, giving shade now the sun was across the meridian. He lay with his chin on dark green water-moss, which grew on and covered a smooth shelf of rock. Cold clear water flowed by him. He rested, lightly, on sand graded to the length of his white belly, motionless while the sand stirred in grains by his grey fins with their pinkish tinge. He rested, away from himself in an unconscious dream of water flowing from everlasting to everlasting. The wounds

on jaw and flank, and the bruises gotten in attempts to ascend the two weirs above Denzil's Pool, were healing.

A few lengths behind him Gralaks was swimming, in the slow current wimpling by water-growing alder roots. She hovered a few inches under the surface. Sometimes the tip of her dorsal fin drew a fine riffle through the undulating reflection of leaves and trunks and sky. And farther down, in shadow by the stone base of the middle pier of the bridge, lay Trutta.

The bridge was hump-backed, built towards the end of the eighteenth century, in an age of the picturesque and landscape ornament among the landed proprietors of England. Water flowed under its three arches and slid whitely into a deep pit beneath. Salar had reached this pit four nights after leaving Denzil's Pool. Immediately above the bridge he had found a lodge, both pleasant and safe, in deep water beside the middle pier. The deep water continued under alder roots and hollows of the bank. Salar explored these, and then swam up the throat of the pool into swifter water, where he rolled in delight. For an hour or more he lay in the run, then he let the current take him, tail-first, over ledges of rock, to the water rebulging from the central pier. There Gralaks was lying, and the two lay side by side, enjoying the clarity and taste of the water, the feel of loose gravel under them, the gleaming movement of trout before them, and the nymphs swimming down one after another. Secure and happy, they enjoyed the river life as little fish again.

Shiner, who worked two days a week in the garden of a house just outside the Deer Park, saw sudden-broad gleams in the dim green water as he peered over the northern parapet of Humpy Bridge during his dinner hour. It was as though first one fish, then the other, turned on its side to scoop something off the gravel in its mouth. In front of the salmon, and to the right in shoaling water, he saw an occasional tiny gleam, not whitey-green and slow like the salmon, but yellowish swift flashes, trout half-rolling to seize hatching nymphs. All the fish were feeding on them.

As Shiner lounged on the bridge, peering down, he wondered how long it would take him to get those fish out; less than a couple of minutes when the water was low.

A week later when the old man went there, the water-level had dropped. The stream no longer bulged back from the piers, but slid in shadow darkly past them. The noon sun shone on the gravel above, revealing every stone and waving green tuft of water-crowfoot growing out of the gravel. Yellow stones were now brown; purple and grey shillets were dulled. Everywhere the algae was growing making the riverbed dark. Larger stones were speckled with the shelters of crawling larvae of flies: little cabins of stone-chip and sand cemented together by the larvae, which browsed on the river-pastures of the algae.

Shiner knelt on the grass-edge under the stone upper parapet of the bridge and stared at the trout and parr lying on the gravel, their black and red spots vivid in the sun. They might have been lying under glass, so still and bright were fish and water. The midday sun was hot on the old man's back, the beams pierced his coat which was ragged like lichen, and the colour of the stone of the bridge. He wondered if the salmon had been gaffed out; he could not see any long blurred shapes in the water. While he peered a trout sprang for a fly, and the ripple-shadows were golden on the gravel. He watched another sidle to a floating leaf-fragment, eye it, hesitate, and then return to its hover.

A few minutes later, as he was washing his hands beside the stream, a thought came suddenly to Shiner that astonished him: the fish in the river must enjoy swimming in such clear, cold water, and they were alive just as he was alive.

Swallows returned from Africa, and flew over the river, gliding down to dip their breasts in the water, and arise dark-forked of wing and tail, twittering their joy of azure air and gliding stream. When next Shiner looked over the parapet, while munching bread and bacon between his gums, the gravel was a darker brown, long strings were tangling out from the crowfoot plants, and dark green flannel-weed was beginning to cover the stones of the shallows. An edge of gravel showed dry and bleached under the rushes of the bank opposite the alders. Many more gravel-speck cabins were on the underwater stones. No trout were visible. He wondered if someone had limed the water at night; that would account for no fish.

All the trout were in the fast run rippling in the throat of the pool. Beside the run horses stood and swished their tails, pawing the loose stones and dipping their noses in water which cooled their feet and swirled by their fetlocks. Behind and beside one another the trout lay, watching for stone-fly creepers which were leaving water for air. From the shelter of the undersides of flat stones the insects were creeping, making for the shallows. Some were washed down, struggling and clutching with their six legs, each multi-hooked, at the gravel. They were miniature flattened alligators, with wide bullfrog heads. Each had a tail of two long, slender prongs. The trout watched

for them, each fish before or behind a stone which gave shelter from the bubble-rushing water: the biggest trout in the best position, the next biggest in the next best position. The best position was where four flumes, each a food-stream sweeping over a different part of the gravel ridge, met by a mossy stone which stayed the quadruple flow momentarily and intertwined them. Thus a fourfold supply of food was to be sucked in there.

A trout of a pound and a quarter, unusually big for that moorland stream, lay with its tail-fin pressed against the stone. Its eyes were fixed on the four-fold twist, which often enswirled a brown, yellow-bellied creeper. *Snap*, and a complex mechanism, in course of changing its motive apparatus from swimming to flying, was sucked into wide jaws, crushed and reduced to fragments, dissolved by acids into a liquid which would be used in building up tissues in the trout's muscles for the maintenance of itself before the stone.

Many times a red-spotted pennant fin showed and vanished in breaking water; the stone-fly creepers, drawn by the lightness of the water, were moving thickly from their retreats.

Once the big trout turned and rushed at Graula the smolt, which had dashed into its feeding place and taken a creeper before the trout had fully opened its jaws for the force of water to sweep the insect into its mouth. Opening its mouth wider, the trout slashed at Graula, who skipped along the water and escaped while the trout, falling sideways after its turning rush, was borne away from its stone. Two other smolts flashed away from the sight of big yellow belly and blue neb. When the trout got back to its place, it found another trout there, one nearly as big as itself, which had moved up from behind the stone. This other trout was driven off, and returning to its place behind the stone, it found Graula there. The smolt slivvered away to another feeding position.

Graula and the other smolts were more slender than trout of their own size. Most of them were two years old, as long as a man's hand. Graula was three years old, and bigger. They were changing their moorland coats for the coming sea-venture. The black and red spots were overlaid by a blue sheen; the back also was blue, and on each gill cover was a purplish mark. The smolts were stronger and swifter than the trout; smaller mouthed, tail-fins forked, bodies more slender for the whip of speed.

Graula remained feeding on creepers until the shadows of the alders lay short in the water; it was afternoon: the hatch was over.

Then the smolt dropped back with the current, passing the root-mass below which lay Gralaks.

Attracted by the lithe gleam of the little fish, the grilse rose and swirled the surface with her tail-fin; an action of pleasure, for the sight of the smolt stirred within her a feeling, beyond memory, of a journey to unknown great waters. The smolt saw the salmon, and a strange excitement played in it, adding to the feeling which had been growing more strongly day after day, as the river carried it from stickle to pool, from pool to glide and surge and run, always downwards to an unknown excitement. So they passed—Graula and Gralaks, two units of the water-spirit, sisters as it chanced: for they had hatched together from a redd above the Fireplay Pool, dug by the same parent, nearly three and a half years before.

The earth and her seas turned from the sun, and the first twilight brought the water-bat from its hanging perch under the middle arch of the bridge, the white owl floating over the grass, and rabbits looking forth from their burrows scrabbled among the roots of the ancient oaks and chestnuts of the Deer Park. Graula was then in the deep pool above Sawmills Weir, hovering on the edge of the fast glide before the lip of the fall, fearful of dropping tail-first into white water, where enemies would be lurking.

In the night Graula went down the leat, with other smolts, and was swept under the fender with the overflow; for the mill-wheel was not working.

When the earth revolved into sunlight again the smolts were lying under a hillside of tall fir trees. On the crest of a Douglas pine stood a heron, gilded by sunrise on a field of azure.

By next dimmit light the smolts were come to Steep Weir, most dreaded by all kelts returning that way, for the river fell sheer from an overhanging irregular lip, to rock beneath, on which the water broke heavily. Only in high spate were clean-run fish able to surmount Steep Weir, by swimming up the solid brown curve of water.

On May Day, when black swifts from Ethiopia were hurtling through the upper air screaming with almost reptilian excitement at their return to the valley, Graula was below Otter Islet and the Junction Pool. The dark bars on her sides, as though inky fingers had clutched her, were silver-blue, and she had grown longer, slimmer, more forked of tail. During the midday hatch of duns the water was everywhere dippled by the migrating schools. Sea-trout smolts moved with them, all their dorsal fins straked with white; the pennant fins of some were single-spotted, others blotched with vermilion.

Their cousins the salmon smolts had no red on their pennants. Down the river they went, Graula among them, under railway bridges and round wide bends, through pool and stickle and jabble and run, and so to the deep Carrion Pit, where the final soft stannic lustre was put upon their scales. They drew the sea into them, they leaped among the first tidal waves, they knew the fear of nets although escape was always sudden swift through the large meshes. Among the strange-ness of seaweed Graula swam, rejoicing in the new food which was so plentiful by the sides of deep rocks.

For a while the smolts travelled with the tides, until one day the river was forgotten, and they went down over streaming gravel banks under The String, meeting place of the Two Rivers; past the weedy chain of the Pool buoy, leaping as the ebb took them under the Sharshook Ridge, watched by fishermen whose unformed thoughts were for the welfare of the little fish. Beyond the lighthouse, white at the edge of sandhills, past the beach where pied oyster-catchers stood thick in flock, under the keels of small yachts heeling to the western breeze, through the tide-rip over the rocks called Hurley-burlies, and so to the tolling bell-buoy, and the open sea over the sandy shoals. There big grey bass, spined of gill-cover and dorsal fin, were waiting for them; and of the sea Graula knew no more.

16 *Shallow Ford*

Under most of the bridges and by the waterfalls of the Two Rivers, small and sturdy black birds, with white breasts, were calling their young from domed nests made thickly of water-moss and lined with dry beech leaves. These nests were hung on ledges or in crevices of rock near the water. Some were fixed in the face of falls, dripping wet with drops; but dry inside. The birds, called dippers or water-ousels, delighted to perch on points of rock in the stream, or bankside snags, and sing to the water. They turned about as they sang, restless as water, bobbing and curtsying; they quitted their singing places abruptly, flying with strong flight, usually following the river course, but sometimes cutting across bends.

When Salar had swum over Steep Weir, a mile above Denzil's Pool, a bird had been flying agitatedly in the spray and thunder of the fall: its nest was in the face of the stone weir, behind the barrage of white water. The dipper had built it during the drought of February and March, when it had flown fearlessly through thin water. For two days the bird had flipped about the weir, crying its sharp watery cries, and on the third day a tree branch had lodged on the sill and split the solid overfall; the bird had dived through to its eggs, cold and white on the beech leaves. Since she had not begun to brood them when the spate had risen, they were unharmed. They hatched out two weeks afterwards, when Salar was settled in his lodge above Humpy Bridge.

There was a dipper's nest under the middle arch of Humpy Bridge. The bird had sat there serenely while the spate was lapping its foundations. Trutta lying at the base of the middle pier was used to black and white flickering at the nest above him. He heeded no longer white splashes in the water, as the bird cleaned its nest before flying away. Trutta had often seen a dipper flying down the river: a blur ploughing the quick-silvery surface, forming into white-black over him an instant before blurring out again.

Every day the water moved slower and warmer, and Trutta left his lie by the cutwater for a trough in the pool upstream. The last sight he had of the dippers before he moved away was four heads thrust out of the side of the nest as the parent flew and clung there, with caddis grubs, and sometimes the fry of trout and salmon, in its beak.

Two days after the sea-trout had moved upstream, Midnight, the black hunter, wading in water under the shade of the bridge, swishing its tail, sniffed at the nest. Immediately there was a brook-chatter of noise, and four young dippers fell out and dived into the water. Midnight drew back in astonishment. The nestlings, who had never before left the dark interior of the nest, swam away from the horse's legs, underwater. First one, then another, bobbed up after a dozen wing-oarings. Their plumage was a greasy blue-black. They lay in the water like miniature cormorants, heads low and necks outstretched. The current took them over the fall, down amidst a swarm of bubbles to a sandy bed wherein sodden branches were

embedded. They oared themselves to the surface, and scrambled out on the rocky walling beside the pool, to crouch shivering in a row, blinking at the unfamiliar bright sky and loud noise of the river. Soon the parent birds found them, and fed them; the noon sun looked in upon the shelf where they were perched, and they ceased to shiver.

When the rays of the sun touched Trutta, as he lay still in the deepest part of the pool above Humpy Bridge, he pushed in under the alder roots, to the brown-green dimness of a hiding place. The movement dislodged many fragments of algae which had been growing on the roots, covering them with a brown slime. The fragments were borne slowly to the surface, lifted by small bubbles glinting on them. This algae was in decay, and the bubbles were of carbonic acid gas. It grew fast in sunlight and heat, absorbing oxygen for growth, and giving off the gases of death.

Everywhere except in the fast runs this algae was growing, rising in fragments with the lightness of bubbles, and floating to the surface. No fish were in the stagnant backwaters where it grew most thickly. Only water-snails crawled there. Between the runs and the edges of still areas of water scores of fry, of salmon and trout, were quivering to maintain position, watching for cyclops and daphnia and minute larvae of water-flies. If one of the fry came too near the hover of another, it was driven away, and within the space of a quarter-second the rightful owner of four cubic inches of water was back in its place, watching for approaching food. These fry were no longer than the top joint of a man's finger. They had tiny red and black spots on their scales. Some of them were already double and triple fratricides.

By mid-May the mossy stone in front of which the largest trout had lain during the hatch of stoneflies was above the water, its top was white where dippers had perched, the moss was brown and dry. Mingled grey lines showed old levels. Amidst the dry moss clung the shucks of creepers, brittle and vacant, each burst at the thorax whence a damp fly had writhed a way into air and sunshine. Male stoneflies had short stub wings, but the wings of females had grown and uncrinkled as they hid on the undersides of stones, waiting for twilight mating.

Sometimes a stonefly, as yet unaware of flight, would attempt to cross to the farther bank, its six legs moving fast as it was spun about in the glittering rapids—a narrow, dark fly, long as one of the salmon fry which darted themselves at it with scarce-perceptible splashes. The fly skated on, suddenly disappearing into a suck-snapping noise amidst the running babble-glitter.

While Salar and Trutta and Gralaks were hiding in lethargy from the glare of the day, other things rejoiced in the water. Bullocks stood in the shade of alders, chewing the cud, meditating coolth and the inanity of themselves. Drawing a line of startling blue down the middle of the river, Halcyon the kingfisher shot through the centre arch of the bridge, seven fry held in throat and beak for his seven young perched on a willow in the pool of Sawmills Weir. Soon he was back again, drawing a line less straight because his flight was rising. He left a cry, hard and keen as an edge of glass, in the shadow of the bridge.

Then daintily flitting, sipping through air as it sipped from water, a slender grey bird with yellow breast and long tail lit on the mossy stone and undulated there, never still but never restless, lilting with colour and movement of water, and calling with rillet voice to its mate seeking stoneflies by the river verge. Men called this dancing bright slim bird a dishwasher! It skipped off the stone, twirled to take an olive dun in air, returned to the stone, danced and rose again, took two other flies and skipped away to its nest under a rock by a waterfall.

When the sun was central in his burning arc many nymphs were hatching. Dusky alder flies crawled laboriously up the trunks of trees and the stonework of Humpy Bridge; yellow sallies ran there hastily, as though in astonishment of their own quickness; olive duns flew up almost vertically from the surface after hatching, to seek the shade of leaves and there to dry the dew from their wings, and await the final brightness of life.

Down to the ford came the glossy hunters, led by Midnight and a little ancient pony. This small horse, thin of leg and neck but otherwise rotund, had wandered about the Deer Park disconsolately, for many weeks, until the hunters had been turned out to graze; then the pony had found a friend. Before their coming it had moved about alone, scarcely able to enjoy a pensioned life of freedom: a mere observer of sheep, hens, pigs and bullocks. But now these high-stepping tail-fleeing lordly ones were come, the pony enjoyed every moment of life, following them at an energetic canter when they paced away at a long trot; and neighing shrilly when they thundered away at the gallop. No longer did it suffer an extended rotundity, caused by indigestion and a dull landscape. It always grazed beside Midnight, by this act most proud of itself.

The horses stood on the stickle, while drinking and pawing the gravel, causing innumerable small stones and specks of sand to move away, disturbing the lives of nymphs, snails, limpets, shrimps, larvae of gnats and other two-winged flies, leeches, fry of salmon and trout, elvers, lampreys, caddis, water-spiders, and myriad differing forms of small life.

One of the pawing strokes of the pony nearly killed a little squat fish called Gobio, and her ninety-seven young, which Gobio was guarding under a stone about as thick as a man's finger and half as large as his hand. Gobio lay still; there was little else to do in life but lie still and pretend to be part of the gravel. She clung with fins like two fans to the edge of the stone, her yellow body spotted and blotched as gravel. When the waterflow became regular again, she wriggled under the stone, to be beside her ninety-seven offspring, which she had stuck to the stone for safety.

Once Gobio had been to Gralaks an apparition with huge open mouth trying to prise away great rocks whither the alevin had hidden for safety. That was three years ago. To the new-hatched Gralaks, her

egg sac yet unshrunken to be a belly, stones smaller than walnuts had been great rocks: and Gobio, little more than an inch long, had been the most fearful thing in the river.

Actually Gobio the mullhead was almost the most frightened thing of the Two Rivers. She was food for nearly everything that swam or dived or peered into the water. Although two years older than Gralaks, Gobio was only a little longer than her pennant fin. Eels were her worst enemies; they thrust their snouts under stones, and writhed to lever them up with their necks—rippling strength turning and screwing and waving while the mullhead resembled more and more the fixity of gravel. The night before Salar and Gralaks had moved into the pool above Humpy Bridge, Gobio had been in dire peril. A big blue-black eel which lived there for the pigs' and rabbits' guts and other things which sometimes were tipped into the river from the nearby farm, was digging for Gobio, when, just in time, an otter had come along. The eel lashed in vain; it writhed itself into a knot of slime about the head of the otter on the bank; all but its heart, near the tail, was eaten. A fox ate the head, later.

Now Gobio was waiting under her favourite stone, to which her ninety-seven eggs were stuck. Within each egg two dark eyes were rolling about, as though signalling to escape. Gobio was on guard, valiant defender against the raids of any caddis or dragonfly larva; and also, a meal ready for any trout, salmon, eel, otter, duck, kingfisher, heron, moorhen, or dab-chick. The stone, and her gravel-coloured skin, were her only protection.

Having cooled their feet and drunken their fill, the horses walked away to renewed interest in grass. The gravel settled again. The last of the hoof-frog scent was carried past the hiding place of Salar. Under the big fish was a silt of decayed leaves and dead weed and residue of old spates. Snails drew their wandering lines through the algae which gave the mud a covering as of velvet. Sometimes from this soft dissolution a bubble shook upwards, the vapour of death. The temperature of the slow eddy rose slowly, and there came a moment when Salar's breathing made him aware of the heaviness of his head; he moved out, into dazzling sunlight, to meet the shock of cold water which made him leap for the pleasure of falling back into an illusion of sea waves. For a while he remained in the run, his back fin just under the surface, and his paired fins hardly clearing the ledge of rock which crossed the river there. Feeling his leap, Gralaks edged out of her hide, and lobbed herself out of the water a few lengths ahead of Salar. Trutta was more cautious; he hovered, with slow sinuations of pinkish-grey tail in shadow, close to the mass of roots which hid him from enemies.

Soon Salar became used to the golden dazzle behind him, the sharp clearness of rock and stone and weed before his eyes, the distinctness of leaves and branches and flying birds over him. He felt uneasy in thin water under the bright sky, and returned to his hide, pushing under the roots until his tail-fin was hidden, and only his head was showing. There he fell into a torpor, breathing slowly, sometimes twice in rapid succession.

For nearly half an hour Shiner had been kneeling by the upper parapet of the bridge. He watched the grey-white mark appearing and disappearing in the water by the alder roots, as Salar opened and closed his mouth. He went back to the garden and told his boss what he had seen, and how the big salmon was "slunging his chine down there in the moots of th' harlder". The old man added that he would be sorry if anything happened to the fish. Then looking at the small globules of greengages forming on the tree spread against the south wall of the cottage, he said, "They birds wull be after they plums in a few weeks; I've got some old netting put back in the shed to my place, I'll bring it along, 'tes a nice tree, and I reckon they old blackbirds can find all the food they wants among the snails and slugs."

17 *June Morning*

Motionless, save for movement of mouth and gills, Salar lay under the mass of dead and living roots. Above the water-roots, and from those exploring the earth of the river bank, arose three trunks of alder. They were lichened; their branches died easily; the alder was a tree that spread itself by earth and water, easily abandoning its injured limbs and offshoots, and creating others.

One of the trunks of the alder under which Salar was sheltering had been dead some years. Its branches were all fallen away from it. Fungus, lichen, and moss grew on it. Many holes of woodpeckers were picked in its soft wood, where grubs had tunnelled. One of the holes was neater and rounder than the others: entrance to a nest gouged by Hackma and his mate, woodpeckers. They were little black birds capped with red, with white-speckled wings. In the nest four young woodpeckers were chissiwissing incessantly. Before they had come into the woody hollow as eggs, while the nest was being gouged, the dead branch of one of the great Spanish chestnuts on the hillside had often resounded with the excess excitement of Hackma; he used its hard core to amplify his drumming song, which sounded as though he were striking the wood with his beak many times a second. But now Hackma's energy throbbed no more between tongue and palate. He was too weary to sing. For eighteen hours a day he sought for and fetched for and filled six (seven were his mate at home) chissiwissing throats in the hollow of the dead alder.

Salar heard the noises of claws and of wings rustling. They were audible in the roots. He watched something moving slowly up one root, and connected the movement with the noises. The thing he watched was like a small prawn, with a pointed tail, grey, crawling slowly up a root from which fragments of algae fell away. It had a plated mask-like head and jaws which had eaten many fry of salmon, creepers, and elvers. During its wanderings in mud it had torn out

141

small lampreys by the tail from the silt in which they lay buried. This creature's life in the river's backwaters was a preparation for solar life of brittle and flashing splendour.

Salar watched the slow crawl up the root and the reflexion of the larva crawling down to meet it, until the two met, merging into one at the scintillant surface, to proceed upwards in the blurr of air. It crept straight up the bark of the dead trunk and as it rose higher Salar saw it clearer, for it was directly above him.

While watching, he forgot the itch in his gills, where small white maggots were hanging, sucking his blood.

The grey crawler stopped under a dried patch of fungus and became fixed there. It did not move; and yet there was violent movement within the shell. Legs, eyes, thorax, body, tail, were being urged away from the fixture of old life by an irritation of power which caused it to strain and twist, until it broke away.

However, its freedom was not yet gained. It was still shut away from the sun which, for the first time in its life, was to be sought, not avoided. Its head, with the rapacious mandibles, was pivoted on the armour of its thorax; and forcing it round within the grey shell, which was becoming more brittle every moment, it bit with its mandibles and strained to reach the sunlight. When the shell was dry it split, and at once a different being began to tear a way out.

Salar watched the head moving outside and getting larger as it dragged itself out of the shuck. It came out backwards, as though to crawl down to the river. After a rest it began again, and pulled itself clear. It walked away, unsteadily, then clung to the fungus with its six legs, which were set with hooks to the knees. It was colourless, flaccid, unmoving; and lost shape in Salar's sight.

The salmon dozed, lying there aimlessly, he who was formed for piercing leagues of ocean, who had leapt away his power's excess in the foam of waves a thousand miles from land. He too was being changed by a Spirit of which he knew nothing except in a dim recurrent rhythm of excitement.

When next Salar fixed the sight of his left eye on the trunk above, an hour later, the brittle shuck was still clinging to the bark below the clot of dry fungus. Beside it was Libellula the dragonfly, a tremulous movement of body and four wings held to the sun. In the first hour of her freedom the wings had sprouted from the buds and uncurled to crinkle as the sun poured its fierceness into their network of nervules which strengthened the membranes. The dragonfly clung

Michael J.Loates

there, wings quivering with waves of feeling flowing to it from the sun.

And while it skimmed there, drawing colour from the golden dragon of the sun, it felt the need for movement, and with a sudden rustle of wings was away on its first flight. Its luminous eyes, with their many facets, quested a crinkling sheen like to itself. Hour by hour it absorbed more colour, until it was an emerald green.

Many times during the days of hotter sunshine Libellula returned to the dry alder trunk, and Salar saw her there, brown against the sky. From above, Libellula was a deep green, with black head and legs. When clouds hid the sun, and at night, she lay quiet, a being neither of air nor water, the metallic sheens gone from her wings, desire gone from her; but when the fiery breath of the solar dragon touched her, she became swift and fierce with the very heat and light of life. Her globular eyes were inpouring with sunlight; they fixed upon other winged flight, her prehensile mask moved forward from her face, she pursued and snapped her prey, clipping off wings and legs and tearing and swallowing.

In flight Libellula met others like herself, and the matings were fierce and selfish as all her life. Wings and mandibles of male dragonflies clashed by her; she drew to herself all who came. Her wings burnt to a darker green; until the fire passed from her, and she clung to the alder below the phantom of her old life, her eyes unfixed from aerial movement, and filled with the vacancy of sky.

Salar watched Libellula clinging there, without interest. The itch in his gills was irking more every day as the river moved slower and warmer. When he had first leapt in the pool the river had been running bank-high; but now it was scarcely trickling over the shallows, where more stones were grey-white with bleached algae.

Soon after the sun had passed the meridian he moved out of the shelter of roots and tried to scrape off the irritation on the top of the water. He was seen below, on his side, pushing his head along the surface, half roll, half leap. His colours revealed his staleness. The back which had been like new-cut lead was now a brownish–blue; pink was tingeing the dulling scales of his flank; and the underpart, which had been white as porcelain during the journey from the sea, was now a yellowish grey, with a worn resting patch at the point of balance. The lower jaw was smudged with black, and greenish with the slime of stagnation. Along the split of the tail-fin were two lines of opaque yellow, and the skin around the lamprey-wound was also ringed with yellow, which was spreading slowly on the dead tissues of the skin. It was fungus, as on the dead wood above him. This fungus disease spread only at night, when the water was cold; warmth of day checked its growth. It grew also along the bony edge of his lower jaw, where the hook had been stuck, and where skin had been scraped against gravel, trying to ease the maggot-itch in his gills.

Salar's shape was slowly changing, too. His head had grown longer, and the kype at the end of the lower jaw was more hooked, so that he could not entirely close his mouth. His skin was thickening, his stomach had shrunk away. He had taken neither nymph nor fly for more than a month. His spirit was depressed and dull as his appearance. Long since the sea-lice had sickened and died and dropped away, and in their place fresh-water shrimps flipped about on his back, sometimes clinging to the fins and nibbling the edges, the salmon unmoving, penned under the roots, in a little shrunken river that Midnight could almost jump across. In the low summer level the deepest water of the pool was hardly up to the hunter's chest.

Brilliant sun: absorption of radiant heat increasing: temperature of water rising above that of air. Not a trout moved, even to flies which fell on the water. Decaying algae absorbed oxygen. All the trout were lying in the fast stickle, where it rippled and dashed and took from circumambient air oxygen which was the life of the river. Salar breathed irregularly; the colder, fresher water did not pass by the roots, but in the middle of the river.

Below Humpy Bridge, below its deeper pool, cattle stood in the shade of alders, knocking tails against branches and hips in torment of gadflies whose low buzz they had heard for the first time that year. The flies settled on their red backs, boring through the skin until they tasted blood; the flies gorged themselves, swelling lazy and content and dozing, to awaken and dig deeper until their heads were liquid. Some fell into the water, to be carried down struggling feebly; trout looked at them, and let them pass. The fish were used to prisms of light, diaphanous wings and delicate touch of waterflies.

Wild pigeons and the smaller turtle doves flew down to the shallows by the run, to drink, and cool their feet in the murmurous water. On long green strings the water-crowfoot waved and twisted, its flowers and buds drowning as the current turned them over; slowly they swung back, untwisting, and white cups of blossom looked at the sun a moment before the water swept them under once again. Nearly every dry stone bore its creeper case, frail and empty, clinging there in still life, wind-trembled.

The salmon waited dull, prisoners of the drought. Other things rejoiced in the heat and light. The white of its breast increasing, the dipper sped down under the shadow of the alders, diminishing sturdy blackness. Other dippers, less white of breast, grey-brown of back, young birds, followed. The leading dipper rose over Humpy Bridge and dived down again to follow the river. When the family had gone, the kingfisher—smaller, faster, keener—drew his straight blue lines through bends and curves: flashing brilliance of emerald and sapphire changing to tawny of underwing as it passed, narrowing blue again to shoot under the middle arch and pierce with silver lancing cry the stone-reflected water-shadow.

Jackdaws with ashen pates, and azure eyes as of heat's insanity, flew over and floated down like burnt paper to the ford, to lower heads and sip and raise black beaks, and fly away with cries less querulously jangling. Old Nog the heron drifted over, hesitated, wheeled on hollow wings, vol-planed down, and alighted on yellow stilt legs upon a grassy mound by the bank. After staring around with bone-splintered sharpness, while the black plumes of breast and head waved against his smoke-grey plumage, the heron stalked into the shallow water where he stood still, blinking at his own reflection wavering and sun-splashed. Seeing the neb of a trout show for an instant as it took a fly, he walked forward, with head down-held, to the first riband of fast water, from under which little shadows darted. He waited for them to return, settled into stillness, yellow-spindled, emaciated long neck extending from humped shoulders, narrow head with its thin black plumes of mock-mourning for death of many fish he struck, but never ate.

After waiting there a couple of minutes, Old Nog saw a change of wavelet shape in the run. He peered lower. A sea-trout, fresh from four months' feeding in rock pools and sandy surf of the coast, after its return from spawning during the winter, had moved into the run. It was the first of the summer run of small sea-trout, and had left the estuary six days before, resting by day and travelling by night. With a precise stroke of slightly open beak the heron stabbed it; with another he held it. Holding it aloft, curving and recurving in struggle to be free, Old Nog walked to the bank, up which he clambered with the help of elbow'd wings, and dropped it on the grass. There it flacked and writhed, while he watched it with a gravity of narrow head and small yellow eyes.

Two crows saw the fish from on high, and flew down. They alighted near, and began to walk around as though they had seen neither heron nor fish. Old Nog ignored them. The crows looked in the grass for beetles, then abandoning the mock-search, stood still, watching the heron; but remaining well beyond the striking range of the beak. One flew up and settled on the other side of the heron. Old Nog gave each a glance, then peered down, picked up the sea-trout, which weighed nearly two pounds, as though it were no bigger than a smolt, and dropped it again, turning it over.

After an apparently careful inspection of the fish—he was really watching the male crow which had walked closer behind him—Old Nog picked it up once more, and let it fall, as though it were distasteful. Then he lifted it and tossed it, caught it by the head, and tried to swallow it. With scissor-beak wide open and legs braced, he gulped. Immediately the male crow flew at him, cawing angrily, and pecked at his eyes. Old Nog jerked the fish away and a grey feathered snake struck at the crow, who avoided the thrust and hopped away, to squat on the grass as though it had never seen a fish or a heron, and scratch its poll with the claw of the middle toe of its right foot.

Again the heron, ignoring the crows, peered at the silver-shining fish, as though examining the close-shaped spots along its length, to which fragments of dry grass and earth were sticking. After turning it over several times, rubbing it along the turf, picking it up by the tail and dropping it again, Old Nog began to break it open, for the amber-pinkish eggs which he knew, from the fish's shape, might be inside it. This was his favourite food, as it was of most living things in the river. The eggs, however, were ungrown, a small mass of orange specks which he swallowed. He was not hungry, having eaten many smaller sea-trout, half a pound and under, at the edge of Sloping Weir only an hour before.

Had the crows not been there, Old Nog would have abandoned the fish on the bank, and returned to the water; but as they were waiting there he stayed too, looking anywhere but at the birds directly. Thus he was alert for instant action. He saw the figure of a man before they did; but the change in his attitude told the crows that a common enemy was near, and they were in the air before the heron was. With circular sweep of wings to push the air behind him, and with scaly knees bent for a jump, Old Nog got off the ground and swept himself away up river.

The man, who was Shiner, shut the Deer Park gate behind him and walked under the tall lime trees towards the bridge. Knowing why the crows had been waiting there, he crossed the river and walked fifty paces to the ford, where he saw the mutilated sea-trout. Thus Shiner acquired a good supper for himself and his kitten—as he called a cat which had lived with him for more than thirteen years.

18 *Mayfly*

When Shiner had gone back to the garden to work, a small bird flew to the river and waited on a branch of alder for something it had seen arising from the water. The bird was a female chaffinch, and its nest was in the fork of an apple tree in the garden, two hundred yards distant. So lichened and mossy was the apple tree, so nobbled and flaked and twisted in its effort to escape its parasites, that the nest had not been seen even by the sharp eye of Shiner. During the second week of April the chaffinch had moulded her nest to the fork, using horsehair, spider-web, moss, feather, and lichen: smoothing the cup in its centre by squatting within and turning round, pressing breast against pleached hair and feathers.

Now eight halves of eggshells lay below, and the young chaffinches were nearly fledged, with nestling down waving on their new and quill-scurfy feathers.

From before sunrise until after sunset every day the hen chaffinch, helped irregularly by her mate, collected insects in her beak, and flew to the nest, where four mouths were nearly always outstretched to take them from her.

The name of the cock chaffinch was Coelebs. He was more gaily coloured than his hen. From various vantage perches he sang a monotonous interrogative song which sounded to the gardener's ears like *Will-you will-you will-you will-you will-you kiss-me-dear?* During the courtship he had repeated this refrain all day; when the eggs were laid he had sung with less excitement; when they were first hatched the quality of his song changed to a flat monotony; and now that the young chaffinches were nearly fledged, Coelebs sang only occasionally, and usually from a distance, and at sight of strange hen chaffinches. The fledgelings knew his voice and song, and listened for it.

During the previous winter he had flown with many other

chaffinches as gay as himself: the Romans, who had observed the habits of cockbirds flying in a flock, gave to the bird the name of Coelebs—the bachelor.

The hen had seen something fluttering palely from the river, and had flown to an alder branch to await the arising of another. She remembered this luscious food from the spring before during her first nesting. Wiping her short, blunt, pointed beak—made for seeds rather than insects—on the branch in anticipation, she looked about her, turning her head to one side for a moment as she heard, from far away down the river, the familiar *Will-you will-you will-you will-you will-you kiss-me-dear?*

A shadowy movement in the river below—which the bird saw clearly to its bed of rock and gravel and dark green moss—made her turn her other eye to see what was happening. A greyness was moving in slow diagonal, with slow waves of tail, into clear water with rippling golden shadow-lines on the rock under. It lost outline as it entered fast water, but the chaffinch saw it there, a shadowy blur, lying still.

Again she cocked her head sideways, to assure herself that the big bird swinging over the valley was not dangerous. *Gor-ock!* cried Old Nog, seeing that the sea-trout he had left on the bank was gone. *Gor-ock!* His craw was tumultuous with two eels, black corkscrews which he had lifted from the river by the carcass of a salmon left, the night before, by a family of otters. The broken fish lay on a sand scour behind a tree-root embedded in the gravel, ten minutes' flight up the valley.

Gor-oo! One eel was trying to move up his gorge. Old Nog did not want to lose the eel, nor did he want his crop continually to be coming into his mouth like that. His cries of indecision were heard by the crows, which had been searching for pheasant chicks and young rabbits in the fir plantations of the hillside, and *kaa-kaa-Nog!* they cursed him.

The heron flew away, and immediately the chaffinch forgot it. The bird's eyes were never still. They looked at the river, at the sky, at the branches, at the troop of horses moving towards the ford, at the sky again, at the water, not fixing sight anywhere yet instantly aware of any movement, which was scrutinized for danger or food. In one of the water glances the bird saw what it had been awaiting: a pale green fly arising from the deeper water beside the run, where rock and gravel were covered by silt. Fluttering to meet the green drake, which arose slowly in spite of rapid wing-fanning, the chaffinch hovered before it and took it in her beak; and away to the nest in the apple tree.

About a minute later the bird was back again on the perch, scrutinizing the undersides of leaves for smaller flies while awaiting other duns of the mayfly to hatch from the silt.

Thereafter at intervals of less than two minutes the chaffinch flew to and from apple tree and alder, taking every green drake she saw. Sometimes she returned as though large-whiskered, with six or seven crumpled and moving feebly in her beak. Coelebs also flew to the nest with bunches of green drakes; but the young birds were sated, they could not keep open their eyes, they sank down one on the other, filling the nest solidly to the brim, so that the hen could not clean it out. Coelebs also was sated, and sat on a branch among small cankered apples, not knowing what to do with his beakful. At last, recalling a hedge-sparrow's brood in the bank among hart's tongue ferns of the sunken lane leading up the hillside, he flew off and put the food into yellow gapes that waved to him as soon as he alighted on the edge of the nest. Having got rid of the drakes, he flew to the hedge-top. Dozing in the apple tree, the hen heard, with only the least interest, his *Will-you will-you will-you will-you will-you ki*—suddenly cease. A sparrow-hawk, silently gliding down the lane, saw him and flung itself over backwards, turned on a wing-tip and thrust out a talon'd foot. A pair of swallows pursued the hawk with ringing cries as it flew away with the stricken Coelebs; but over the river they turned back and dived down to the water, to cool their breasts and sip; and flying back, they caught each a floating coppery breast-feather for their nest in the rafters of a cowshed.

While the hen chaffinch was dozing uneasily on the heads of the fledgelings, sheltering them from heat with wings spread over them, and while the swallows were playing with feathers in air, another mayfly was about to appear out of the stream. Danica, pulling herself from the nymphal shuck which had split as she reached the surface, shook the creases out of her new wings, and found herself arising, with the strangest feelings of fear and wonder and joy, to a shining freedom.

Spotted gold gleam and splash was a trout leaping at the pale green cloudiness of light moving upwards, steadily, to the shelter of leaves. There Danica the mayfly clung, twisting her body, with its tail of three whisks, in release of joy which poured through her eyes. On long and slender legs she walked from the leaf to its stem, and thence to the twig, and remained there, her body curved upwards to the sky, and her wings, pale green and diaphanous, drying in the warm air that moved through the trees.

Libellula the dragonfly, in final fury of hunger, with brittle rustle of wings passed by and saw Danica, paused, then swooped to take a blowfly whose coarse buzz made lambent fire of her eyes. Libellula was possessed with a frenzy; she was heavy with eggs; feelings burned wildly within her; the dark green of her wings and body was almost black, sun-charred. She ripped the wings off the blowfly and champed it, but could not swallow. Dropping the hairy blue shell, Libellula fluttered to the waterside, lighting on alder roots by the base of the dead trunk on which she had hatched.

The westering sun threw shadows of trees half-way across the river. Having refreshed himself in the sun, Salar went back to his hide in deep water. He did not push under the roots, but lay beside them, concealed by shadow, in water that moved slowly and gave easy breathing. And lying there, he watched Libellula rising and falling over the little bay of still water, at each fall touching the water with the end of her body. Minute after minute the dragonfly stabbed the water, each time dropping an egg; nearly two hundred eggs a minute sank down to the silt.

After a short sleep the hen chaffinch returned to the alder, and seeing no mayflies hatching, began to hop from twig to twig, peering under the leaves. The bird saw Libellula below, but the colour did not attract her. She searched the leaves, taking ephemerals of large and blue-winged olive, and flies of willow, alder, and hawthorn. Since no more green drakes were hatching she sought away from the still water of the outer bend, at each return visit flying nearer to the bridge.

Danica rested on her twig, feeling a dry tightness about the now familiar airiness of herself. This was because the pellicle, or fine skin which enveloped every part of her, was about to split down the back. Then Danica would be to herself all beauty of sky and water. For this final losing of herself in love the unknowing nymph had toiled in the silt of decay and darkness, feeding on diatoms, little vegetables of the river: now she was a spirit in resurrection, without appetite, her mouth sealed, needing neither food nor drink, a being of beauty and light whose doom, or reward, was to die in the sunset of her day of aerial life.

The pellicle broke, and Danica was transformed, her wings clear and iridescent.

Pale blue-grey, empty, the fine sheath from which the mayfly had flown trembled on the twig in a wind too slight to stir an alder leaf. The afternoon sun gave a brazen light to the valley, with lengthening shadows of hilltop oaks extending in advance of a general shadow. Leisurely the horses walked down to the bend to drink; there were fewer gadflies to worry them. Swallows dipped and wheeled and rolled over the grass; higher up swifts raced in a thin black chain, crescent-linked. Above them Danica was flying, in a tiny cloud of her own wings, palest grey. Near her another mayfly, streaked black and white, with large luminous eyes, was flying. When Danica had floated up the sky, the black drake had been flying with seven other males by the parapet of Humpy Bridge, in a rising and falling formation: they were spinning, flying up and pausing, to drop with closed wings, to rise again, one close by the other, spinning their racial dream of imminent and immortal life. When Danica had arisen, the black drakes had followed her, rising into lucent sky until but one was left to pursue.

To the moon's pale phantom flew they, to find in sweet shock the everlasting river. Then they were falling, apart, the black drake empty of hope and illusion; the grey drake to the winding gleam below, bearing thither a strange secret joy.

Over the river many smaller flies were moving; some in shifting dark clouds, tiny dark flies, two-winged, called fisherman's curse, since trout preferred them to other flies, and they were too small to be imitated in silk and steel and feather. From the bridge the black drakes were gone. Other ephemerals were spinning there—pale wateries like little white ghosts, blue-winged olives and iron blues, their delicate legs and whisks trailing, iridescent with the hues of sunset and decline.

Salar now lay in midwater, idle, without movement, his chin resting on a ledge of rock, nearly asleep. He had seen Libellula the dragonfly fall at last into the water, struggle feebly, and be carried slowly away.

Gralaks moved from her shelter, and lay beside Salar. Three leeches hung to her tail-fin. A trout with a dark thin body and large head sidled past them, and hovered under the surface, watching for one or another of the dark cloud of flies—they had hatched from the shelters of sand and gravel-speck which encrusted most of the larger stones of the river-bed—to touch the water. The trout was dark brown and thin because its gut was filled with a thread of worms, a dark brown family joined together in a string, male to female, female to male. So numerous and flourishing was this family that its youngest offspring were hanging, desperate and miserable, outside the trout's vent. The head of the family was secured by hooks to the lining of the

Michael J.Loates

fish's stomach; it was this head that absorbed most of the fly-juices before they could be passed to the trout's liver. Thus the trout was starved and lugubrious.

Another trout moved into the run spreading out with bubble and foam patch into the slower water. It had been sleeping in the shadow of one of the arches of the bridge, and during sleep its golden-yellow hue had faded into vertical bars of black and yellow, a pattern of protection. Within a few minutes of being in sunlight again—for the hill-shadows were not yet half-way across the valley—its red spots had changed from scarlet to vermilion, the dark bars had faded, and the fish was again its gravel-bright self.

A salmon's length above Salar, another trout was lying, in its early evening place: a slight saucer-like hollow in the rock. This fish was dark green on its back, resembling the water-moss which grew on the rock. Near it lay a smaller trout, almost lemon colour, hue of the fine grains of sand which sloped down from a lip of rock, its usual feeding place when the spinners came on the water towards evening.

Shadows of alders crossed the river; the water was cooler; floating bines of crowfoot ceased to give off oxygen. The air was yet dry and warm; swallows and swifts played in the upper sky, where a lone herring gull was tumbling and twirling among them as it took spinners in their nuptial flight.

Rings of ripples began to spread on the river. The clouds of fisherman's curse had ceased to drift and sway; black knots moved slowly, as though aimlessly, midges in marriage. Two pairs of wings upheld the union, until one partner faltered, and the little mass of life sank down, to touch the surface, and struggle, and vanish in a lip of water spreading in a ring of ripples.

Side by side the two salmon lay, watching the flies, but inert to move. Some distance below them, in the deep pool cut by the triple falls of the bridge, lay Trutta, under a pink curl of bubbles which stroked his purple head. Not for Trutta the slime and stagnancy of roots; he was way-wise in the river; this was his eighth return from the sea. Behind the pug, in the deepest part of the pool, adding to its floor litter of rotting leaves and sticks and bones, a large eel lay twisting brokenly: an eel thick almost as a man's wrist, blue-black head and slimy back. Until an hour ago this eel had feared nothing in the pool; it had fastened on to salmon kelts and hung there, eating the sick and living fish alive, bite by bite; it had drowned ducklings, dragged down full-grown dabchicks, pursued dippers, and eaten two or three trout every day. But when—the colour of the old sea-trout's skin having suggested a sick fish—it had swum up behind Trutta and bitten between dorsal and pennant fin, it had the enormous surprise of being chased about the pool and, as it swam into its hold under the stone-facing of the bank, of being seized and pulled out, gripped in teeth and spat away, seized again and shaken, and then being gripped across the middle and held there while it twisted and lashed in vain; and only when Trutta had crushed it into two pieces, still joined but writhing independently, was the eel free to move whithersoever it pleased.

Trutta lay under the cascade, waiting for dimmit light, when he would swim up the water slide and join Salar and Gralaks in the run above.

As he lay there, ruddy light lifted from the cascade; the sun was behind the trees on the western hill.

In the coppery glow still brimming the floor of the valley the spinners were burnished points until they dropped into shadow: they were thin streaks of sunset fire rising to fall vanishing.

To the dipper speeding in relayed jerks upstream, the water had the colour of the sky, a leaden whiteness; while the kingfisher cutting downstream across a curve flew amidst a vast hue of its own breast.

High overhead the lone gull flew, slowly into the day's end, silently flying to the headland of the west, to the sea murmurs and cliff cries of its brethren.

A bead of gold was shrunk bright on the coppery glow of sunset, Venus the evening star. At the zenith, the sky was pale and clear: its pristine azure was cold with starlight journeying from distant night-suns before salmon leapt in the Island Race, before mayflies rose from water, before the sea grew bitter with earth's dissolution.

When the sun had gone under the hill Danica rose from a leaf whereon she had been resting, and flew down to the water. She was azure-pale as space, a fleck of sky fallen and dancing over the river. Lightly she touched, paused to drop a cluster of eggs, which sank to the bed of the river as she flew up again, to dance over the ripples, to fall again to her own wraith rising to meet and embrace her from the water.

Brighter shone the evening star. Another heron passed in the height of the sky. The roar of the triple falls grew louder under the bridge in dimmit light. Her gauzy wings and body becoming grey as passion ebbed in her, Danica danced away her life's day, while the water-wraith called to her, and she sank to a last embrace, and floated, wings spread and head down, under the arch of the bridge, and fluttering feebly, was borne over the fall to where Trutta watched and waited, resting on a rock within which was a mayfly set in stone a thousand thousand years before.

19 Night Sun

As Nirra the water-bat flittered from her cave under the bridge, a wave arose from the smooth river and travelled rapidly downstream, as Salar leapt and smacked down on his side. The sight of the great pointed head so sudden near made Nirra loop and flitter back to the arch, in fear for her baby clinging to her breast. Nirra rustled into a larva blow-hole in the stone, and licked the black head burrowing hungrily into her warmth. Two grey horns of lime hung from the mortar which bound the stone of Nirra's home, inverted pillars for the doorway. They were not the wrong way round for Nirra, as the water-bat always hung head down when resting, delousing herself, or biting and being bitten by her mate, Nirro. For the past moon, however, Nirra had been at peace, except for her lice. Nirro had vanished shortly before the birth of the batlet, and thereafter no high petulant screaming and grinding of needle-sharp teeth had been heard coming from the larva-hole.

Another splash, as Gralaks flopped half out of water, across the slow-moving current. Nirra was accustomed to the noise and sight of the big splashes in that place at twilight, and flew happily over the water, flitting in sudden stoop and return, snapping midges and moths, and sedge-flies which had hatched from underwater homes built variously:—of minute pebbles, diminutive empty shells of water-snails, fine sand and stones in the shape of turrets and pinnacles; or from cabins made of silk to which were fastened twigs, stems and stalks of buttercups, and dead leaves. At the end of each turret or cabin was small grating, which let in water but kept out enemies. Thus the caddis lives until the time when it bound itself completely in silk and slept: to awaken into flyhood, bite a way from the cocoon, swim to the surface, break from its special swimming suit and emerge a sedge-fly ready to instant flight.

The night-flying sedges crossed and recrossed the water, while

Nirra snapped, and tumbled as she put the insects in the pouch of her tail.

The bat saw Salar and Gralaks swimming just under the surface of the water, side by side. They were released from the glare and fear of day. Salar's tail-fin idled out of water; it was more brown than grey. Gralaks swam away slowly, turned on her side, and tried to rub the itch in her gills against the stones. The grilse gleamed a yellowish green in several sideway slidings along the river-bed. Salar swam around slowly, and then went down to scrape the sides of his head on the stones, showing broader gleams of worn silvered copper by the grilse's tallow-yellow. The bone of one side of Salar's jaw was worn rough, where he had rid himself of the hook two months before; the place still irked him, where fungus had its hold.

Soon the feeling of elation sank in the two salmon, and they rested on the stones, and mused on the green twilight of the water as they waited for the glowing hues of darkness.

A splash, a shake in the middle fall, brown back-fin and tail-tip zigzagging up the glide; a ream drawn through the shadow of the arch: Trutta had joined them. His flanks were dark-spotted, currants and raisins and cloves; his back marbled rufous and green. He could not quite close his mouth because of the thickening of the kype of his lower jaw.

Trutta moved up into the run of fast water, and Salar followed him, with the ease of confidence; and while the sea-trout lay at the head of the run, the two salmon half-rolled and played in water scarcely deep enough to cover their backs.

Nirra the water-bat was now flittering erratically near the surface of the river, after flies which had come there for warmth: the air was colder than the water. Invisibly in deepening twilight swifts sped, their shrill whistles faint in the height of the sky. The dark heavy shape of a wood owl appeared on a branch of alder, and with a squeak Nirra rustled into the larva-hole, zeedledeedling her alarm to the batlet, who continued to nibble a teat in sleepy play, unaware of what its parent was declaiming. A swelling appeared in the owl's throat, and a hollow cry bubbled from its open beak. It saw the gleams of the salmon below, and the phosphoric glow of fungus on Salar's side and tail-fin; it saw every spot on Salar's gill cover: for the owl's eyes were large, each iris blue like a grape with bloom. It saw the sedges and the moths, some dark red and others cobalt; a duck's feather floating down glimmered; a water-vole gnawing the root of a rush on the farther bank was grey, although by daylight its hair was dark brown.

The owl jumped off the branch and vol-planed down with legs hanging and toes spread; the vole also jumped, *plop!* it was in and under the water, and the owl was perching on another tree, peering down for small fish moving there. In the past it had taken trout and salmon parr in its claws; all movement caused its irises to expand, liquid grapes with softer bloom.

As soon as the owl had flown away a wild duck that had been waiting in the still water beside the middle arch of the bridge quacked discreetly for her ducklings to follow, and paddled upstream. Hardly had she gone beyond the angular cutwater when she turned silently and swam back beside the arch, the nine ducklings quiet beside her. The duck had smelled something in the cold air moving down the river.

A fox had slipped across the grass from the edge of the fir plantation on the hillside. It stopped on the bank to assay the air, and then crept down to the ford to drink. First it must smell the hoofmarks of the horses, each one very carefully, as though its life depended on no strange horse having joined the herd since its nasal inspection of the night before. Satisfied with the familiar scents, it drank a little, then withdrew from the bank to sniff about, as on second-thought, possibly to discover a stranger which had not drunken, but stayed away from the river lest it leave scent there for the fox to detect. Finding nothing new, it raised its sharp snout to flair the breeze before slinking over Humpy Bridge, to follow along the other bank to the broken bay, where damp sand and silt held the press of many more hooves. The fox learned that pigs had been wallowing there during the day; and also that a dog of strange scent had visited the ford to drink. This was alarming, for it could not recognize the smell; so after wetting it, thereby removing the smell from the earth and the doubt from its mind, the fox went away, satisfied, towards the hen-house and the rabbit warrens by the avenue of chestnuts.

A soft quacking under the bridge: having smelled the fox away, the wild duck paddled upstream beside the pier, followed by nine ducklings nearly as big as herself. They had come from their day-haunt in the deep tree-hung pool above Sawmills Weir. The duck had made her nest of dry grasses in a higher fork of a mossy oak, twelve feet above the water. The lower or main fork of the oak was bare of moss; an old dog-otter lying there during the many summers had worn the bark smooth. The otter had been killed by hounds a year before, but the moss had not grown again on the rank place. One by one, when they had dried after chipping out of their shells, the ducklings had been carried to the water, held between the duck's thighs. Every night, now that they were nearly grown, the family travelled up the river, eating snails and caddis in the backwaters and eddies, and turning over stones for creepers of stone-fly and march brown, and fry of trout and salmon.

Under the bank by the alders the family paddled and splashed and played. The smallest duckling had a habit of climbing out on the bank and standing there on one leg, its head sunken on its shoulders, in an attitude of sleep. Then, when the rest of the family had gone upstream, the duckling would queep loudly, causing the duck to delay further progress and gather the others about her, while she called the truant to her. Night after night the small duckling did this, and always at the same places.

Salar did not see the ducks going upstream, for they moved in the still water of the bend, by the opposite bank. Nor did he see the white-flipping tails of a family of moorfowl following discreetly after the louder ducks. The cock and the hen led the way, followed by the four remaining and grown birds of the first brood, and then by six smaller birds of the second brood. Three of the first brood were hens. These looked after their six small brethren; but the fourth, a cockbird, had no interest in anything except feeding itself.

When the ducks and the moorfowl had gone upstream, Nirra the bat flittered alone in the darkness, clasped by the batlet, now exploring her body. Nirra talked to it in squeaks sharper and higher than the needle-notes of mice running over the roots of trees, with their litter of old leaves and twigs of bygone spates. Larger moths were now fluttering over the river, their wings sometimes striking against the alder leaves; spiders were on their webs; stars shone in sky and water. Venus was gone, far beyond the Island and the rim of ocean; the moon leaned on the hill: Night was come to the valley.

With the sinking of the moon came full darkness, and many things began to glimmer on earth and in water. A pale green wandering fire in the grass was the love-light of a glow-worm, herself wingless, beacon for some dark-flying rescuer. Trees were a deep velvet blackness. The pole star held its fixed light above the Plough; northwards the sky had the pallor of ice. As the water-bat flittered between starry river and starry sky, it heard and saw what was now a familiar thing: the noise of iron rolling on iron, and the ruddy dilations of fire on steam. Far up the valley a late train rumbled across the viaduct.

Salar felt the distant vibrations in the rock. He lay in the run, behind Trutta. Both he and Gralaks, behind him, were watching for food, but only the sea-trout was feeding. Salar had the illusion of continuing a journey to the unknown and final heaven of his being: for which he had travelled from deep ocean to the Island Race, and thence to the estuary and the higher reaches of the river. The river was no longer a stagnancy of warm, betraying water; it flowed fast and keen, glowing with life.

After lying there an hour he became restless, and turned and swam back to the deep water, to swing again into the current and hover just under the surface. Then forward again, slowly, seeking fast water. He saw the rock glowing darkly red under him, the luminous wings of moths, the deep-blue-blackness of the alder roots, the brown and green hues of the gravel. Some floating objects passing on the glimmering surface were seen darkly; others shone with colours. A cast breast-feather of a heron, grey by daylight, was now a rich red; while one of the white breast-feathers of a dipper was a dim black. He saw the alder trunks lambent, crooked as with moon-fire.

At midnight the solar rays reflected from the middle of the Atlantic laid an ocean pallor along the western sky. The Plough, seven points of light, had swung round the pole star. New constellations arose as the western stars of nightfall set beyond the hills and the sea. Sky, rocks, water, glowed with the fluorescence of their own dark lives.

Salar and Gralaks lay in fast water, close to the tail of Trutta. The water was running cold from the springs in the rock of the moor. A stag which had been lying with other red deer in the spruce plantations of the hill came to the ford to drink. It crossed below the fish, which neither saw nor heard it. The stag walked across the park and up the hillside, making for a hedge where the young leaves of ash and ivy were to its liking.

Just before dawn, when the density and coldness of the water was greatest, a strange salmon moved up beside the others. This was Gleisdyn, who as a smolt had migrated to the sea with Gralaks fourteen months before. He was longer and deeper than the grilse; the extra ten weeks of sea-feeding had made him four pounds heavier. With other grilse who had escaped the nets in the estuary, Gleisdyn had come up the river, running at night in the thinnest water, and resting by day. As the face of Steep Weir was dry, with docks and other plants growing in cracks of the stone of the sill, Gleisdyn had not come to it; he had followed the stream running into the river-bed lower down, overflow from the raised fender by the mill-wheel.

Swimming through the mild gush of water under the oaken barrier, he had followed the stream up the leat and into the millpond, past low muddy islets to fast shallows under tall trees, and round a bend into deep water, following the way of the spring salmon in April. Three miles above Steep Weir he had come to another side-stream, which also led under a raised fender, and into another leat. This carried the water from the millpond to the wheel of the sawmill; the fender was open to release the water when it was not working. So with the least effort Gleisdyn had entered the pool above Sawmills Weir, which, like Steep Weir, had been dry.

Gleisdyn swam into Sawmills pool just before midnight; and two and a half hours later he reached the water above Humpy Bridge, and saw Salar and Gralaks. He had left the estuary four nights previously, having come in over the bar during the weekly close-time, when netting was forbidden, from midday Saturday to midday Monday. The sea-lice remaining on him were only just alive.

Stirred by the white and silver of the stranger, Gralaks swam down the run, throwing herself out of water. Gleisdyn followed, and after a while Salar drifted down tail-first, turning as he reached deep water, and accelerating, drove in beside them. They were half-rolling around one another in play when Trutta swam down, and turning, sank to the deepest part of the pool, and lay still.

Alarmed by his attitude, Salar and Gralaks ceased their sporting, and lay behind him, in mid-water, moving their tails nervously, like small trout hovering. Trutta lay still as a stone. Gleisdyn half-rolled beside Gralaks, and then, turning in alarm as he saw something, shot away in an immense ream or wave, towards the piers of the bridge. He slashed round in fear of shallow water of the glide, and returned, piercing his own ream. The wavelets slopped against the bank, while the four fish lay motionless, inert, on the bed of the deepest part of the pool.

Trutta had been startled by the glimmer of surface movement coming upon him rapidly. The wild duck and her ducklings were swimming so fast downstream that they appeared to be running on the water.

Less than a quarter of a mile above the ford was another waterfall, by tall beeches which had been planted when the fall was built for ornament. The family of ducks had been happily bobbing and flapping and talking there, all of them in the water, except the littlest duckling. A flat stone leaned in the pool below the fall; and on this the littlest duckling had been perching, on one leg, feigning sleep, when the duck had started to quack loudly and beat her wings for running flight down-river. The others immediately followed her, but the ninth duckling remained perched on the stone. To turn attention of the otters from him to herself, the duck returned and splashed about in the shallows, dragging a wing as though wounded; but soon the cries of the duckling ceased, and terrified by the musky smell, the duck flew down-river to pitch beside the others and lead them in the race for distance and safety.

They saw the gleam of turning fish, and heard the drumming vibration as the salmon speeded away. Through the western end of Humpy Bridge the family hastened, sliding and bobbing over the white water, moving like a broken string of large oval beads in the shadow of the stonework, slithering round the roots of an alder, and down the noisy stickle of broken shallow water.

A low whistle, softer than the cries of flighting curlew, came from above the ford. The otters were coming.

20 *Water Death*

An hour before, while the stag had been drinking at the ford, the dog and bitch had met by chance in the Fireplay Pool, just below the railway viaduct. They had not met for five months, since just before the cubs had been born in the marshes of the river-head.

The dog had been travelling up the river, after salmon shut in the low pools; but before coming to Humpy Bridge he had gone up a runner or streamlet, remembering the eels there. The bed of the runner, which trickled at the bottom of the garden wherein Shiner worked, was alive with stick-caddises, therefore of mullheads; and eels went after the small squat fish, burrowing under stones for them. The otter's best-liked food was eel. The claws of his forepaws were worn small by scraping under banks and large stones. Sometimes the otter-hounds drew up the runner; but it was boggy and shut in with undergrowth and scrub, and the huntsman in consultation with the master soon decided that hounds were hunting heel—that the otter had come down the runner, not gone up it.

Many times the man living in the cottage, for whom Shiner worked, had heard the soft, water-musical cries of otters travelling up the coombe. The otter lived all of itself, and so spent many hours in playing and whistling.

Usually the otters quitted the thread of water at the head of the coombe, crossed fields and went down another runner which joined the river below the railway viaduct.

The dog-otter, working down the second runner while the stag was leaving the fir plantation for the ford, heard the cries of otters playing, and hastened after them. In the deep slow water of the Fireplay he met his mate, and the cubs he saw for the first time. The bitch had a white patch of hair on her pate, in the form of a star; her dam, who had died toothless during the last winter in the Seals Cave of the headland, had had a white tip to her rudder. The bitch's sire had

Michael J. Loates

been a bold otter who, after being hunted many hours, and escaping from worry after worry, had drowned a hound with his last strength. His name was Tarka.

At first the cubs were scared of the big strange otter. He caught a trout wedged in fear under an old pail filled with cement, and left it for them on a shingle bank. Soon they were playing merrily as before, wrostling in the water and rolling together down the narrows and cascades, and sniffing beside his wide jowl at the scent of ducks on tufts of rush and riverside scours. They went down with the river, and heard the roar of their first falls, echoed from the beech trees. The old otters had often played there, falling over head first and climbing up to slide down again, whistling their joy. As they went over this time the dog sank away in the white rush and when the cubs went over they fought around him, to seize the duckling which was flapping and crying at the base of a leaning stone. They tore its wings off and left it only when it was dead, to frolic after the bitch calling down the fast thin water.

It was nearly night's end. The fox, returning from the bracken of the rabbit warrens, heard noises at the ford which sounded like horses crossing. Webbed feet and thick pointed tails were striking the water as the dog and the bitch clutched one another and struggled in play. Seeing nothing, the fox was puzzled and anxious. It lay down, flairing its nose to smell the reason of noise. Made most curious, it crept slowly towards the alders, ready to run at the first sight of danger.

In the deepest water lay the three salmon, motionless with fear. Trutta lay some way behind them, on the edge of the waterfall. When the short-legged beasts came darkly into the dim cone of fish vision, Gleisdyn turned and shot away, followed by Salar and Gralaks. The otters heard the thumping vibration, and separating, swam down and peered around with swift movements very different from the heavy clumsiness of their play movements. Before, they had been land beasts sporting in water; now they were of the water. They became longer, slimmer, their heads sharpened. They tucked in their forelegs and swam seal-like, swimming about with sweeping movements of tails which had become rudders. A gleaming form drove suddenly between them, turned with a roaring noise, and after it had vanished they were lifted by water surging solid under them. Gleisdyn, not knowing the river above the bridge, was rushing about in terror, his accumulated sea-strength stripped from him by shock after shock.

Salar and Gralaks were sunken on the gravel at the base of the western pier of the bridge, as though made of lead.

Trutta was hidden under the largest mass of roots, where Salar usually lay by day. The pug was afraid, but he knew what he was doing. He lay still as the roots, one flank protected by the bank. He was ready to move from whichever way the enemy should approach.

Gleisdyn drove downstream from two large and four small dark enemies. His bow-wave smacked against the two piers of the middle arch when he was ten lengths upstream again. In a thruddling zigzag he shot through the pool, swerving from one otter and throwing himself out of water to avoid the bubble-glimmering turn of another. He slid along thin water, driving a furrow in the gravel.

As the bitch, neck-hair raised, leapt with purring growl upon Gleisdyn, he threshed a way past her into deeper water, and sped upriver. The noise of his ploughing up the run made the watching fox trot away from the alders and turn back again, ears upright, nose and whiskers twitching.

The dog-otter bobbed out of the deeper water, and stood on the surface a moment, on his webbed hind-feet. In several quick movements of his head he fixed the glimmer of fish and bubble travelling upstream, and as he fell back with a splash, called the others to follow.

Gleisdyn sped up a gorge between rock and gravel where the river hastened round a bend. He passed a small groove in the rock, and returned to it when he learnt that the river spread thin over shallows above the bend. He fitted his length into the groove, and lay still.

The dog, swimming upstream from side to side and bobbing out of the water to breathe and peer every few yards, passed Gleisdyn and, coming to the shallows, ran out on the bank to listen for the noise of the salmon's passage upstream.

Meanwhile one of the cubs had found the fish, and had scratched it timidly with its paw to see if it would move. The next moment the cub was swallowing water as it gasped from a blow which caught it across its middle and hurled it against the rock.

Gleisdyn had not struck the small otter deliberately. His strength was going from him in shock after shock of fear as he fled from sight and smell of one or another of the otters. Twice more he went down to the bridge, and upstream again, followed by a wide wave. On the third rush downriver he came face to face with the bitch, whose teeth as he slashed round bit into the wrist of his tail. His momentum tore him free, and in wildest fear he swam up the run again, driven by the feeling that he must get away from the ford. Past the gorge he arrowed, and soon was threshing amidst flat stones and thin water, desperately driving himself forward, breaking his skin on sharper edges of larger stones. The otters ran upon him, curled their hairy-spiked necks over him, clasping the cold body with their stumpy forelegs and slicing off scales and skin with their teeth. Curving and slapping as he escaped, Gleisdyn writhed to the water, but the dog caught him by one of the fore-fins and dragged him back, rising up and falling upon him to tear flesh from the thick part of the shoulder. Soon the large bones of the back were exposed, and the fish bled to death. When it ceased to move they left it, for they were not hungry: this was their sport.

The fox had been watching, a coming and going tall-ear'd shadow on the bank, during the hunt. When he was satisfied that they were gone—for once, and once only, he had questioned an otter walking into the badgers' sett which the fox had taken for his own earth—he crept down over the stones, shaking first one delicate pad, then another, as it got wet, and sniffed carefully along the entire length of the salmon. After a long interval, during which the chase was reconstructed by sense of smell to its satisfaction, the fox braced his legs and set himself to drag the carcass to the bank. This was done after some slipping; after which the fox kicked his heels against the grass and shook his coat. Then he nibbled a piece of red flesh, tasted it thoughtfully, looked round for the otters, walked away as though uninterested in the meal awaiting it, rolled on the grass, wetted a dried patch of cowdung to conceal his own scent, and returned to tear away mouthfuls of flesh and swallow them in lumps which soon made his throat dry and thirsty.

The otters went down the river, passing Trutta lying under the roots, and sliding over the middle fall of the bridge into deep water below. The sky was growing pale over the eastern hills, and they did not linger, but let the stream take them down the valley, under a road bridge, and to secluded water where branches of trees hung over the river, sometimes dragging at the stream. Through the slow stretches they swam, six flat whiskered heads pushing each a watery arrow from its nose. At the beginning of the long pool above Sawmills Weir the dog left them, crawling out by the roots of an oak whose leafy branches stretched over the water to the farther bank. After sniffing round the base of the tree, which was half hollow, and leaving his blackish-green spraints on a root beside other faded marks of bitten fishbones—relics of former visitations of otters—he climbed up the sloping trunk and lay in the fork, where he had not slept for nearly a year. After licking his hair and washing paws and face, he curled to sleep, as a cockerel crowed in the garden of one of the cottages beyond the sawmills.

He left again before sunset, and went down the river, couching at dawn in the thicket of the islet above Steep Weir. There a few hours later the otterhounds found him, and hunted him for four hours, and caught him at last, very tired, in shallow water, even as he had caught Gleisdyn, and slew him.

While the otters had been killing Gleisdyn, Salar and Gralaks had gone down under Humpy Bridge and through the pool, swimming fast, often with backs out of water, down the shallows until they came to deeper water, where they swam easier, but always downstream. Only when they came to Sawmills pool, with its deep pits, and shelter made by willow branches dragging in the water, did they pause and swing into the current again.

Day after day they lay in the dim light of deep water. Day after day the water flowed slower and warmer. Plants of celery and hornwort growing in the shallows toppled with their own weights of green; cattle treading the ford higher up broke off strings of crowfoot, which floated until they caught in snag or stone, to put out small white roots for holding. From their base on Humpy Bridge new blackberry brambles stroked the water; sow-thistles grew there, too, with hemp agrimony, hart's-tongue ferns, water-violets, and yellow flowers of mimulus at the edges of rock and river. All had grown there from seeds left by spates.

The lime trees in the Deer Park were murmurous with bees at the blossoms; heavy thunder clouds—travelling quarries of the sky—trundled over the moor. Village boys swam in Sawmills pool, white bodies and brown legs and arms moving slowly and irregularly, with much shouting and splashing. At night mists, hiding the stars, moved over the river and the meadow short with aftermath of cutting.

One afternoon of intense air-heat, as Salar lay asleep under the clogged willow boughs, he awakened to a thudding and agitation of the water. He saw much shapeless movement on the bank of the meadow. The other side of the river was dark with trees growing on the steep valley side. When something shook the willow branches, he sped away, up the river, but turned at the sight of many men and horses, some of them in the river-bed, where the water was only a few inches deep. Something ran staggering and plunging down, wading slower as the water deepened, and swimming.

It was the stag which had come down from the fir plantations to drink at the ford every night when Salar had lain above Humpy Bridge. The stag had been roused some hours before, to run many miles across fields to the moor, trying to outrun the staghounds which followed its scent everywhere its slot pressed. Eventually it had come back to the valley and the river, running down two miles of water, sometimes clambering out to make a loop, and then returning to the water which bore no scent. But the huntsman knew the ways of deer; and now hounds had come up to the stag at bay in Sawmills pool.

Salar fled up and down the pool, alarmed by the swimming legs of hounds. Shiner, standing among horsemen on the bank, saw Salar drive between the dark green weeds on the gravel at the mouth of the leat, and watched his bow-wave hit the iron doors of the fender.

The stag was turned by hounds from the deep water, and as it walked towards the sill of the weir the huntsman shot it with a pistol. The bullet pierced its shoulder. The stag paused, and walked on. The huntsman fired again. A dark spot opened on its neck. It shuddered, and lurched uncertainly, its head beginning to hang, its tongue lolling, blood thickening in strings from its nostrils. The huntsman fired again. The stag stopped, swaying on its feet. It was dead. Hounds bayed around it, while the whippers-in waded to the stag, to keep off hounds. The stag's head, with its thirteen points, dropped forward and its knees sagged and it fell over in the water.

The mill-wheel was locked, no water passing; the smaller fender of the overflow, by which Gleisdyn had swum up, was open. It sucked Salar down, to a little brook beneath. In the shadow of brambles and hazels he drifted, tail-first, coming back to the river again, to a small pool and then another pool in smoothed grey rock. His life was suspended by reawakened shock; his wound was open again; he let the river take him. In the night he went down the leat of Steep Weir, and by morning he was in the Junction Pool, where listless fish lay in water nearly stagnant.

After noon a thunderstorm broke over the moor, and a freshet came down, flushings from half-dried bogs and marshes, warm and turbid water saturated with gases of decay, from which the salmon turned. By morning the river was at low summer level again, the dark algae on its gravel thickened by a fine silt.

The next day a summer visitor was drowned in the estuary of the Two Rivers. He was bathing, at low water, at the junction of the tides. They ebbed quietly away in a string of foam, taking the body with them. It was a Sunday afternoon, and the weekly close-time for nets; but that night, towards low water, all the fishermen were on the Ridge, sweeping with nets, to take the body, they said. Forty salmon were caught. Salar saw one of the nets, and remembering, swam away fast. When the sun arose over the mainland, he was in the bay, and feeding on prawns and sand-eels. That night he lay, with other salmon, a few river-stained like himself but most of them fresh from the ocean, in the tides of the Island Race.

BOOK FOUR

Book Four: Winter Star Stream

21 Drowning World

At the equinox, when summer and fall shared a day of rain that dissolved all colours of land with the moving greyness of sea, the highest tide of the year moved up the estuary. Neither sunrise nor sunset were seen. The grey day grew duller in the afternoon; the waves, piled up by the south-west gale, rolled bigger and slower.

An hour before high water the sea flow ceased, checked by the volume of fresh coming down the river. A brown lagoon lay between the sea-walls strewn with froth amidst branches and roots of trees, drowned chickens, cabbage leaves, and the scriddicks of old tide-lines become flotsam again. It rose until the water was level with the top of the walls, brimming above the grazing marshes. At the hour of high water the wall-tops were weirs, marshes were flooded, cattle floundering and belving, sheep drowned, the marshman in the bedroom of his cottage on the sea-wall watching water lapping the lower stairs.

The day was darkened out long before nightfall. As the tide began to move back the wind dropped, and rain fell straight and black. The clouds burst over the hills and the estuary. Trillions of water-thistles arose on the wide lake of the marshes. Mallard and shelduck flighted in from the sea, joyfully to discover the new world. Shops and cottages of the village beyond the Great Field were flooded. Eels ate the dough in a baker's ovens where fires had burned an hour since. Two cormorants sat together on the gilt weathercock of the church spire above a jabble of brown water hiding tombstones. A heron fished from the radiator of an abandoned motor-car on the new concrete highway, perched beside the mascot of a miniature heron in white-metal. Later, the heron was found drowned: in over-excitement of the world becoming water and the annihilation of Man it had struck a grey mullet between operculum and gill, and unable to free its beak, had been dragged into the water by the fish eight times as heavy as itself.

The lighthouse beam was invisible across the estuary. As the tide pressure ceased, the fairway became a mighty rushing river. Row-boats above the Long Bridge of the town were filled with water thrown over their bows, torn from their moorings, and taken nearly so far as the Island in what was still the river: brown water, unsalt, thick with the soil of many fields.

There was no estuary: only a new great river, muddy and very fast, claiming all its old courses and beds used and disused since its beginning. Everywhere the resurgence of its primitive spirit was hostile to the work of men. At night the town by the Long Bridge was without light, its engines and dynamos bedded in smooth brown mud. The rain fell heavily all night; and all night the engineers worked in the power-house, wherefrom at dawn came the beat of engines; but also at dawn the tide pushed the water over the quays and embankments again, and into the power-house, washing away barriers of sandbags and replacing the mud which had been removed.

Railway lines rusted. Culverts were torn away. Trees which stood for centuries on the river's banks were uprooted and carried down, to lodge against the arches of the Long Bridge, to collect lesser trees and bushes and form dams which made a vast lake above. For years some of the town councillors had urged the making of a lake there, for both power and pleasure: now they had it; but the river had the power and what the councillors called the unruly elements had the pleasure—seeing, among other things, the Town Bandstand going out to sea.

A herd of porpoises, led by Meerschwein, went miles up the river after the runs of salmon which old men said were the greatest ever known. For days, as the river ran lower and clearer but still with many times its normal autumnal flow, salmon were seen leaping in the wide, water-gleaming valley.

Nearly a hundred hours' continuous heavy rain had filled the underground lakes of the moor so that every spring was gushing. Sunken lanes—tracks worn deep by sleds of olden time—were noisy with cascades, their rugged surfaces washed away to reveal rock grooved and worn by iron and wood and horn.

As the flood withdrew from field and ditch and hollow, many fish were left in closed pits and shallows. There was a saying in the country of the Two Rivers that in a bygone age the agreements whereby boys were apprenticed to moorland farmers had a clause which stipulated the feeding of salmon to the boys on not more than three days a week during a year. This saying was often repeated in books of the familiar kind which are derived from other books; but no such agreement had ever been found to prove the truth of the saying, which was intended to show how in other ages Atlantic salmon were as numerous as their Pacific cousins were in later times in the rivers of the Coast.

In the Great Deluge by which Salar returned to the stream of Red Deer Moor nearly all the pigs, dogs, cats, and hens of the valley farms which remained alive turned away, after three days of feeding, from the flesh of salmon. Some said the sudden immense volume of water running into the Atlantic was so charged with the salts of artificial fertilizers washed in the soil from fields that most of the fish coming to the Island Race were unable to find the sea-currents of their native rivers, and so all followed up the one overwhelming waterway to the Two Rivers.

Michael J Loates

Below Sloping Weir the bed of the turning eddy was covered by salmon, which were covered by a second and a third layer of fish. The water of the eddy was a dark purple. Every moment the circular racing surface showed a brown tail-fin, a dark rolling back, a lead-grey or copper-brown neb. Fish six and seven together were trying to get up the weir. At the side of the concrete apron, where Shiner stood, small trout and sea-trout leapt and slithered on the watery slope so frequently that he could, he told himself, have filled a bucket any moment by simply holding it there.

But Shiner was not there to get fish. Now that he had regular work he was quite happy watching them. Indeed, he felt the secondary feeling of all conquerors towards a subjected race: an attitude of benevolence and protection. Shiner had no gaff in his pocket. He was there because most of his life thought with the way of salmon. All day he had stood there, watching them. He ate no food; his hunger was to see the fish.

Shiner's arrival at the weir had disturbed Old Nog the heron who had been killing every fish it could strike and lift from the edge of the slide.

So many peal—small sea-trout—were leaping and falling within a few inches of the grassy edge that soon the old man's trousers were wet to the knees with the splashing. The female peal were long and fine. Some were seven or eight inches in length—fish which had migrated to the sea as smolts five months before, and found scanty coastal feeding. They were lilac-coloured, unspotted. Others were silvery over their spots; these were the brown trout which had found a way to the estuary, and returned for spawning. The sea-trout were all of one family, although in most the desire for ocean was inherited, not an accident. All had had white flesh before going to salt water, but now their flesh was pink from eating prawns and shell-fish.

A few salmon, the tired ones which had remained in the river since early spring, tried to get up the weir at the side, leaping among the smaller sea-trout whose water it was. Shiner saw fish with long heads and out-thrust kypes, brown as summer algae, the gristle of underjaws worn by rubbing and ringed with fungus. They sprang from the edge of the broken surge which slanted across the pool's circle: some fell on their sides, heavily on the concrete covered by water less deep than their bodies, and lay stunned a moment before being washed down; others jumped too high, falling on the curl-over of white water and being flung back before recovering poise and swimming down with easy stroke of tail-fin. Other stale fish had green on gill covers, their jaws looked smoke-grimy, their scales rusty. They were all shapes and sizes. The pool was more fish than water, fish flushed with the cold fever of spawning, all trying to get to the redds in the higher reaches of the river: danger for themselves but safety for the alevins hatching in the shrunken waters of Spring.

Every minute several fish leapt askew and fell on the grass beside the concrete. Shiner eased them back into the water, wetting his hands lest his touch scald the sensitive skin. When he had arrived at the weir-side that Sunday morning, a thistle had stood beside a dock, both growing out of a crack in the concrete; but during the morning both plants were so beaten by blows of falling fish that at midday their stems were shredded from their roots, and washed away.

Nearer the roaring centre of the weir, stronger fish were jumping. Most of them hit the water and lost impetus before they could grip and bore a way up the slope. Shiner saw roseate hog-backed fish, with heads of canary-yellow: these were males of a late run, full of zest for spawning. They had no appetite for food; excitement had released much uric acid in their systems, which gave their skins the livid colours.

Other salmon were pink-silver, others flushed a deep red. One very big fish, a fifty pounder, which had been returning to the Wye, ploughed up the slope, a plume of water curling over its head. Two-thirds of the way up it was in water falling with its weight and strength: it swam with all its power, seeming to vibrate in green glass: then it was moving back, always swimming hard, until suddenly it gave up and was swept down to where the glide was shattered and tossed in ragged white peaks. The sight made Shiner feel in his pocket for a gaff, and then he sighted, for the confusion of feelings within himself.

The spawning coats of the salmon were varying as their shapes and weights. Shiner saw fish that varied from light brown to the colour of bronze, greenish as though corroded by the sea. These were the females. A few clean-run bluish-dark fish had net marks on them; although the official net-season had ended with August. Fish were jumping at all angles, some to be thrown over backwards immediately, others to strike the water and be swept and tossed away. A few straightly entered the narrow central spine, to find, as they swam with all their strength, the under-layers of water which, dragging against the stone of the apron, delayed the thrust of the over-slidden top water. They moved up, flattened images of fish vibrating within green glass.

They made such slow movement because the weight of the top water, pressed by the gliding and swirling masses above the sill of the weir, was many times the weight of each striving fish. The water was alive with the spirit of salmon-life. It was the master-spirit which had given salmon their shapely beauty, and their speed. The pointed power which in water could burst through netting strong enough to support the weight of a man in air, could not pierce the massive violence of the spate. When the water fell, they would go over, one behind and beside the other.

But while he watched, and as the sun broke through clouds, Shiner saw a fish leap from the midst of the most broken turmoil—a curve of white and tarnished silver which fell and pierced the surge and moved up steadily, vibrating fast and surely, a fish that had learned a way through the varying pressures and water-layers, beside the glassy spine raised from the gap in the sill above. It got nearly to the sill, where it seemed to hang, moment after moment, then it was advancing, inch by inch, to where the spine was flattened just below the break in the hidden sill; and as Shiner watched, it shot forward out of sight, to leap high from the calm deep water of the mill-pool and reveal, in the moment of rest at the top of the curve, a soldered mark on its side, as of a wound healed. Such was the return of Salar—the Leaper.

22 *Steep Weir*

As the fed heron flies, Steep Weir lay about six miles above Sloping Weir; but the journey was longer for fish. The river wound through the grazing meadows of its own past making—now running close to the feet of hills yellow and red and brown with the colours of leaves' failing life, now winding to the other hillside; to recoil upon itself, in wide pools of currents in confusion, rushing swollen and gleaming.

Steep Weir had been built in a past century, diagonally across the river, a barrier of slabs of rocks raised and mortared vertically ten feet on the rock. The top layer of slabs overhung a vertical wall; water falling over fell clear of the wall's base. And it rebounded, because it fell direct on rock. There was no pool underneath, no deep water from which a fish could take off. It was the most harmful weir in the country of the Two Rivers, and, since it was usually unpassable, a favourite place of poachers when fish were running.

Where the sill of the weir stopped, a bank grown with alders continued to a half-rotten sluice. This consisted of a frame of three upright posts, bedded into masonry and morticed on cross-pieces. In the grooves of the upright posts two doors or fenders had not been moved for more than thirty years. They were ruinous, and silted on the higher side.

Early one morning Shiner went to Steep Weir. He knew that some of the chaps from the town would be there, snatching fish. Since he had come to watch salmon for their own sakes, Shiner had appointed himself a sort of honorary elusive water-bailiff. Herons and otters and snatchers he regarded as half-enemies of his own life. Water-bailiffs were enemies of the other half of himself, and when he saw one Shiner became elusive. He muttered to himself, feeling they would not believe that he was by the riverside for the sake of the fish. Not for the sake of the Conservancy Board, which was made up of men there to represent and serve their own interests: nets-men for the increase of nets and extension of time to net, rod-and-line men to increase the number of fish in the rivers, by keeping the number of nets as low as possible, and limiting the season of estuary fishing. Shiner knew all about the Board; and he muttered when he saw a bailie, for old time's sake and also because he was a solitary.

Shiner had a special grudge against the water-bailiffs. Recalling the number of fish he had snatched from below Steep Weir, he now thought of salmon jumping there hour after hour in vain, bruising and breaking themselves. Why hadn't they bailies seen to it that the fender was raised? 'Twasn't proper! Very well, he, Shiner, would do it himself.

Soon after sunrise on the Monday morning he climbed over the fence by the road bridge below the grist mill, and walked along the river bank. He was tall and thin, looking like a humanized alder trunk. His coat was shredded and grey like lichen, his arms and legs long and loose. He had a small face with pointed goatee beard and high pointed ears sticking up beside the upright brim of a very ancient and discoloured billy-cock hat. His eyes appeared to see nothing, he never turned round, or glanced about him; yet he saw all he wanted to see. He was a grey heron of a man, owning only his clothes, a few gardening tools, and himself. In summer he often slept out, beside ricks or in lofts of cattle sheds. He knew white owls which nested in the barns, and they knew him. He liked wandering about alone, in the open air. During winter he lived in a room over a disused stable, for which he paid rent of ten shillings a year. He insisted on paying rent. The landlord, an innkeeper, allowed him to boil and fry in the rusty grate of the small disused harness room, hung with cobwebs. Shiner's only mate was a cat, an aged beast, which he called Kitten. It was the great-great-grandkitten of the original cat he had owned. He neither begged nor borrowed, nor would he claim an Old Age pension: he hoped thereby he would escape notice. His secret fear was that in extreme old age he would be destitute, and put in the Union, when he would not be able to see the river or the fields.

He walked along by the river, slowly, with an ash-plant nearly as tall as himself in his right hand, continually glancing at the water moving almost bank-high on his left. Forward, and across the river, stood a plantation of thin trees almost hiding the mill-house. He heard the roaring of the weir as he walked on. A raised bank of stone and earth, on which ash and other trees grew, was between him and the weir. Peering through a gap, he saw the figure of a man standing there, and recognized one of the gang which had stolen his trammel net in the police court. Then he saw the hats of two other men moving behind some low-growing furze bushes. The river was over the bank beside the sluice, running down the grass, and pouring over the edge into the race-way below.

Moving to another gap, Shiner stared at the weir. Fish were jumping into the white, to fall back again, and be tossed and turned in the churn of water rebounding from the rock below. They were jumping all the time, and most of them were coloured in shades of red and brown. "They'm in full tartan, surenuff," muttered Shiner, using a phrase he had heard years before from a visiting Scots fisherman.

In a bed of rushes fifty yards above the weir Shiner had found a rusty iron bar while poking about there a few months previously. This, he guessed, was the bar by which the fenders had been lifted up years before. But if he went to get the bar now, and started to open the fenders, he might be pitched into the water while he was doing it, and no one any the wiser. They chaps wasn't worth twopenn'oth of cold gin, they would pitch him in if they thought no one would know. And taking red fish, too! Why, the eggs of a ten p'un sow-fish weighed two p'un! 'Twas no sense in it, snatching full ripe fish.

Shiner had taken many hundreds of fish at Steep Weir, and had often stated his opinion that October fish tasted better than clean springers; but that was when he had been younger and "lived for devilment", as he said. But a full ripe fish! 'Twasn't no sense to it.

After wondering for some time what he could do, Shiner clambered over the gap in the bank and walked, looser legged than ever, towards the men. The man standing back from the water saw him casually, and paid no heed to him. His two mates had been informed, however, of the approach, and when they saw who it was, they bent down and withdrew each a long ash-pole which had been hurriedly thrust into the growth of bramble and alder.

The poles had been cut from a near-by copse. To the slighter end a noose of twisted strands of brass wire had been tied. These were for tailing the fish waiting below the sluice.

Shiner went to the edge of the sluice which joined the water-roar at the base of the fall a few paces distant. Fish of all lengths and shapes and colours were jumping vertically under the spread of the weir. None could get up. One great fish—it was the fifty pounder Shiner had seen the day before at Sloping Weir—fell back on a hidden pinnacle of rock and was washed away belly upwards. Shiner cracked his fingers, and muttered to himself.

"You won't do nought with that li'l old rabbit wire," said

Shiner. "I was working here with a gaff when Adam was a proper pup. Besides, you'm too late. There ban't enough water here to carry the fish over. Now if you could open the fenders a bit, to let some good water under, you'd attract the sojers upalong the gully." Soldiers was the poaching term for red autumn fish. "Aiy, midears, that's what us did in th' old days. And if I don't misremember, there be a bar lying about yurr somewhereabouts."

He began to mooch around, peering under bramble clumps and kicking tufts of grass with his boot. He returned to the others, mumbling half to himself, "You med get a fish by fixing a gaff on t'other end, and cutting the stick in half, maybe you'd get a vish thaccy way, but you med be careful, midears, leaning over all that water, 'tes a turrible master weight of water valling today. Aiy, it be, too true it be." And shaking his head, he ambled away, pretending to be looking for the bar. "Th' old fool be wandering i' th' 'ead," said one of the men, lighting a cigarette. Seeing this, Shiner came back, talking in a broader, old-fashioned way. "I minds th' time when us took vower butt-loads of vish from thissy place. But then us had th' bar vor open the sloos, do 'ee zee?" and shaking his head he went away. "Proper mazed fool," said the young man, inhaling deeply of the fag.

Shiner was staring at the fenders of the sluice, his billy-cock pushed over one ear, scratching his head. Jets of water were spurting through holes in the oaken planking, and gushing underneath, hissing white from the pressure of water above the fenders.

As he watched, a small sea-trout slithered up the white hiss of water, and turning by the wood, slithered down again. "You'll soon be upalong, midear," said the old man. "Shiner knoweth."

He found the rusty bar in the nettles, and returned to the sluice. An oak plank stretched across behind the framework, and on this he stood, pushing the end of the bar into an iron notch. Each fender was the shape of a large square shovel, in the handle of which was a vertical row of notches. Levering against the cross-piece, he tried to raise the fender. It was wedged in the lower grooves of the posts, held tight by the weight of silt against its other side. By crashing the bar against the plate Shiner at last shifted the wood and immediately the gush below changed to mud colour.

He shifted the end of the bar to a lower hole, and raised it another notch. Thus slowly one fender was raised; then he began to raise the other. While he was doing this one of the men came to him and asked him how much more he was going to "rise" it. "Hey?" said

Shiner, pausing to put a hand to ear, and then bending down to lever again. The man shouted at him, soundlessly in the roar of water now passing under. "Hey?" said Shiner, pausing a moment. The man came on the plank and bawled in his ear. "If you open it to the top, you bliddy old vool, all the fish will rin through, won't 'm?"

"Aiy, you'm right, midear," replied Shiner. "B'utiful water, b'utiful rinning water!"

"I said to you, you old vool, I said, You'm letting all the vish dro, ban't you?"

"No, I ain't got no gaff," replied Shiner, lifting the fender another notch. "If I had, you should have it, midear."

The man seized the end of the bar. "Stop, wull 'ee?" The second fender was almost as high as the first.

"Aiy, you'm right," said Shiner. "Only don't you go telling they old bailies that I was a hacsessry after the fack of this yurr raisement o' the fender," as he inserted the end of the bar into the last hole.

Michael J. Loates

The second man now stepped on the plank and gripped the bar. "What's the flamin' bliddy idea?" he shouted. "Here, you give the bar to me—" and he raised an arm with clenched fist while pulling with the other.

"Yurr, take it," said Shiner, suddenly thrusting the bar at him.

The man who had shouted had been braced for resistance; he lost his balance. He clutched at the other man, who in turn grabbed the third man. The trio leaned back, swaying and clutching. The weight of the bar pulled the first man askew, and all three fell into the water. Instantly they were swept down the race. One got hold of an alder bough in the eddy by the curve of the race, the second held to him; but the third man was carried down into the main rush of the river. He could swim, and so kept his head up. He was washed helplessly down river until he found himself in a backwater. Shiner, who had been following downstream, helped him out.

When the three were together again he said, "You'm a proper double couple o' Adam's pups! Goin' givin' an old 'un like me a proper scare! And where be the bar you was so anxious to get hold to? Like as not in the flamin' sea by now. And I can't reggerlate no fenders just as I was preparin' to do when you wild bathing boys thought you knowed best. I tell 'ee, midear, they be wedged tight by now, and nothin' will shift 'em. Hullo, hullo! Did 'ee zee that li'l b'uty? My Gor, 'twas a b'utiful sight!"

A salmon had leapt out of the white curl-over below the open fenders, had pierced the green glissade descending and had swum through, a dark shadow vanishing. Above in the pool it leapt again—Salar.

23 *Sawmills Weir*

Shiner walked up the valley, beside the river. He did not hurry. He stared and quizzed and wondered. The cottage garden where he worked was under four miles from Steep Weir, and there was little to do at the fall of the year; and Shiner was not the sort to make work. He was a free man. It took him all the forenoon and two hours after midday to arrive at Sawmills Weir. There a gamekeeper saw him. The gamekeeper was also a local preacher.

"Up to your old games, I see," was his greeting to Shiner.

"Aw, you must have second sight, midear," retorted Shiner, looking at the water. "How be the fezzans this year? Got this yurr grouse disease from Scotland yet?"

"You'm a smart one, Shiner, you be. Got a gaff in your pocket, by any chance?"

"You got any baccy in yours, midear?" countered Shiner.

"I ban't a smoker, you knows that."

"Nor be I."

"Then why do 'ee ask?"

"Aw, just another idle gossip question, midear. Hullo, did 'ee see that g'rt old black poll? Proper old berry-gatherer, I reckon."

Garroo the cannibal trout, who had hidden with Salar and the others under the roots when the gang had worked the trammel in Denzil's Pool, had just jumped and fallen back. He was lean and thin; his head was the shape of a lobster's claw. He looked like his own effigy in a glass case; for his spots were large and very distinct, the red very red and the black very black, while he glistened as though newly painted in hues of blue and brown, and over all a high gleam of varnish. Garroo was too old for spawning, but that did not prevent him from doing what he had done for many years: joining in the general excitement of migration upstream, and gorging on salmon eggs—whence Shiner's description of berry-gatherer. The keeper,

189

who knew almost nothing of fish, thought the old man was merely stupid and garrulous. His Lordship did not fish; and his Lordship's agent always let the fishing to tenants. Shiner knew this; he had no ill-feeling against the keeper.

"Maybe a master g'rt wind after frost will blow away the leaves for 'ee soon," he remarked, changing the subject to suit the keeper. "I see'd many young fezzan chicks as I was in the swamp tilling tetties (potatoes) for my chap this spring. Th' ould birds eat my cabbage plants, but us don't grudge them a bite or two, sir. Live and let live, my chap saith: all complaints at the Judgment Seat. He be proper mazed about salmon, writing a book about'm, he did tell me, so I bin and opened the fender down to Steep, you'll see no more snatchin' there, like I used to do before my guts dried up."

The keeper looked at Shiner with a new interest. Shiner, knowing this, began to speak about the fish which were trying to get up the Sawmills Weir. He pointed out how salmon made many attempts to feel the weights of the water; that they were not jumping

every time they showed. They were feeling their way, time after time. Different parts of the weir suited different sized fish. Directly below them salmon were showing, half leaping; but none would try and get up there, said Shiner. That was the small sea-trout place, where the school peal got "up auver".

The weir was built in a series of steps or ledges descending; the water fell from ledge to ledge, toppling in ragged violence. A salmon appeared to push itself out of the lower white and to swim up in foaming water: actually it was slithering on mossy rocks which gave it a good grip. But the water there was too broken for its length, and it fell back, to lie in a trough in the rocky bed below, beside three other salmon which were touching; and over whom the bubbled water raced. The middle fish was Salar.

"'Tes no good for a large fish, just down there, you'll see," said Shiner. "But the li'l tackers go over for a pastime." Almost as he spoke a sea-trout long and nearly as narrow as a man's fore-arm shot out of the white at an angle of forty-five degrees and appeared to fly through the spray at the leaning angle, to alight on a hidden step of rock two feet under the sill, and cling there with its fore-fins. They saw its tail only; its body was beaten by the hard white water. It was pounded there for nearly a minute and then flung itself off the stone and swam vertically up solid falling water, moving gradually up to the bend over the sill and then, with a flick of its tail, it shot forward over the rim. It skipped out a dozen feet away, in exuberance of feeling.

At the other end of the weir the water plunged with more ragged violence off a large flat stone midway between upper and lower river levels. Below the foot of the weir, at this place there was depth for the take-off. New salmon arriving at the weir moved up the main stream which fell from the end where the two men were standing. Only when they had failed many times to reach the lip of the weir did they explore across to the other side, and find, after many trial jumps, the right way up.

"That be the place, my li'l dear," cried Shiner, to something in the water under the far end of the weir. The keeper looked at him with amused tolerance. The old fellow was proper mazed, he thought.

A salmon had shown there, turning on its side. It was Salar, who had arrived at Sawmills at the same time as Shiner. Immediately on arrival Salar had moved into the leaping-off place, and sunk to rest. He let the water seethe over his head and tickle the underpart of his body pleasantly. Salar did not like breathing bubbled water any more than any other salmon; but he lay there easily because, although his body was enswirled and stroked by bubbles, his mouth was thrust into a crevice where water welled in the dark green moss as from a spring.

After enjoying the highly-oxygenated water for a while, Salar moved back with the churning strakes and sank down to the bottom. There he balanced himself under the fog of bubbles. Above him the bubbles hissed; under him the rock rumbled. He lifted himself off the rock, felt the rhythm of power along his muscles passing into the water. He gaped faster at the water, while the flexions of his body rippled faster. He fixed his sight above the fog of bubbles, and sprang; but checked at the last moment. Shiner saw him, a fish of new-cut lead and new-cut copper sliding up moving snow.

Salar had checked on a sudden doubt. The doubt was due to the change of his nature, a change which had been coming slowly all the summer, delayed by return to the sea and renewal of feeding, and now was hastening upon him with the season of coloured leaves and sap sinking in trees and plants. His nature was drawing into itself; he lived more an inward than an outward life. He had no interest in moving things, food, while he was swimming up the river; but when he rested, his old nature returned upon him, and he was irritated and stirred by smaller fish swimming above him and by leaves and twigs and other movement. He took many pieces of black water-moss in his mouth, holding a piece sometimes for a minute or more before expelling it. Then all interest in moving things, which might have been food, was gone; he would sink into himself, his power withdrawn to give colour to his body—skin and fins—to lengthen his head and give strength to the hook of his lower jaw. His skin was thickening, a pattern as of green and brown and yellow marble scrolled thereon.

A confusion of personality had checked Salar's jump; but after another rest he gathered himself and swam up and leapt, to be shocked by the warmth of air, and to fall beside the stone and swim up against the blank gush of water. He knew the way, and swam more strongly, reaching the straightness of the wall at the back of the weir, two feet from the top. The water gushed off his back, and then he was lying beside the wall, parallel to it, in a narrow trough no wider than himself, and well under the curve of water.

He slithered along, and then found he was lying behind the tail of another salmon. The tail was dark brown. This was one of the grilse which had followed Gralaks into the river.

In front of the small fish lay two other salmon, one a yellow-headed cock-fish with a porpoise bite out of its tail-fin: the other was Gralaks, who had been washed down the falls by the flood, and now was making her way up again.

Soon afterwards a fifth salmon wriggled up and rested its chin behind Salar's tail. An almost continuous line of salmon, hidden by the curve of falling water, was now lying directly under the sill of Sawmills Weir.

When Gralaks, the leading fish, was ready to go over the lip of the weir, she slewed her tail round so that the falling water beat on it. She lay between two mossy slabs of rock. She curled her tail for a jump; she sprang; her flanks gripped the hard descending mixture of air and water with scale and caudal fin; she bored upwards with nose and eye and gill and all the determined strength of life being urged forward. She slapped the water with sideway sweeps of her body, and then she was gone, her passing over the lip of the weir revealed by only a momentary bulge in the smooth bend of water.

24 *The Redds*

High over the valley the last swallow was hurled in the wind which streamed the leaves from the oaks and kept the tall spruce firs of the hillsides swaying in slow wariness of grey clouds of sky. By the river the bullock paths were pitted and splashed yellow, under alders dispread black and bare. Over the viaduct a miniature train moved in silhouette, creeping across the sky, antiquated goods trucks on webbed wheels swept about by scattered steam.

From the top of the hill, reddish brown with larch and dark green with spruce plantations, came little reports flattened away by the wind, the first pheasant shoot of the year. Old Nog the heron was trying in vain to outfly the winds over the hill. Higher and higher they took him, turning and slanting and flapping without forward movement, scared by the reports of guns which he thought were all aimed at him. When a thousand feet high he gave up and swung round, and swept across the valley; but a report louder than the others, coming direct to him in a pocket of wind, made him tumble and turn and fly into the wind once more, determined to fish in future only in the wide safety of the estuary. Old Nog had made this resolution a hundred times before; he always forgot it when out of gunshot.

Within the river many salmon and sea-trout were moving. The sluice at Steep Weir was gone; posts, doors, framework weighing more than a ton, had been jostled to the sea, no more to the river in spate than a few twigs and leaves. Already barnacles were laying their eggs on the wood, beside the jelly-sacks of river-snails' eggs killed by the salt.

Every tide brought in more salmon, which reached Sawmills with their lice still alive, four days from the sea. The gravel of the river-bed was stirred and shifted by a myriad changing weights of water pouring around and eddying from fish on the move. And by mid-November, when the river level was steady with fast water running clear as glass, the gravel was being cut up by the tails of female fish—from the Carrion Pit to the runners on the slopes of the moor, streamlets scarcely wider than the step of a boy—salmon were preparing to spawn.

Gralaks lay above the Fireplay Pool. The roe which had been growing within her all the summer were now one-fifth the weight of her body. She was ripe, ready to drop her eggs. Three male fish, knowing this, were near her, waiting to shed their milt on the eggs. One of them was Salar.

Behind the three cock-fish lay Garroo the cannibal trout. Behind Garroo lay two smaller trout who had tasted salmon eggs before. And lying close beside Gralaks was Grai, a salmon parr weighing two ounces, who had fallen in love with Gralaks with all the volume of his milt, which weighed one-tenth of an ounce. Gralaks was aware of Grai; indeed she was pleased by his nearness. Grai knew the other fish were there because of Gralaks, but his feeling for her, especially when she lay and hid him, was stronger than his fear. Grai was determined that no other cock-fish should lie beside Gralaks.

No other cock-fish had yet noticed Grai.

At nightfall Gralaks moved slowly forward on the level shallows above the throat of the pool. At once Salar and his two rivals moved behind her. She turned on her right side and sinuated in an arrested swimming motion, lifting by suction a few stones, which fell back with the stream. Watched by Salar and the other cock-fish, Gralaks settled into the slight furrow and thrust herself into it, to widen it.

During a pause in the digging Grai darted forward from beside Salar's left pectoral fin and took up his rightful place beside the mighty mistress of all sensation. The swift movement loosened a mistiness into the water behind the parr's tail.

The effect of this milt passing by the gills of the cock-fish was one of action and turmoil. One turned and slipped over Salar, and with open mouth made as if to bite the salmon on the other side of Salar, who drove at him, also with open mouth. The three-sided chase rocked the water of the Fireplay.

All during the night, at intervals, Gralaks was digging the redd for spawning—sweeping the gravel sideways and scooping a pit in which she lay. Another hen-fish was doing the same thing ten yards above her, and two more, each attended by one or more males, were working in the fast water between the tail of the Fireplay and a larger and deeper pool below. This was the Wheel Pool. It was wide and round. The stream entering it divided into two streams, one turning left-handed and continuing the main course of the river under overhanging oaks and past sombre yews, the other turning to the right and running back under alders until it was slowed by meeting the main run again. Sticks borne on this flattened circle rode round and round sometimes for months, shut within the backwater.

A ridge of rock lay across the middle of the Wheel Pool, and under this rock, with other quiet fish, Trutta was lying. The quiet fish were salmon new from the sea, and unaffected by the movements of the red fish, which had come into the river months before. Their greenish coats were still untarnished; they would not spawn until the end of January, when the redds of the spring fish which had spawned would be cut up again, and the eggs, dark-spotted with eyes, swept away.

The Wheel Pool was Trutta's pool. He had spawned in the run between the Wheel and the Fireplay seven times. On this his eighth visit from the sea, however, Trutta had not yet begun to share the general excitement. There was still a dark ring round his neck, although the black collar had gone. His kype, which was immense, had grown sideways, and looked to Shiner, who at noon climbed one of the oaks to look down into the pool, like a reversed clay-pipe held in the pug's jaws.

At night the stars were clear and large, frost-sharpened. Tufts of withering rushes and grasses and thistles were rimed with hoar-frost in the morning. Sunrise over the hill of fir plantations was a flush of pink and gold; a clear sky all day. Again night glowed with stars above a mist of frost settling on bracken and grass and branch. The water was colder, and fish did not move much.

Salar, lying behind Gralaks, saw the stars above him with the quietness of his other self. He became alert with the rumbling in the rock under him; and saw the water in front of him glow with fire, which gleamed on the back of Gralaks. High over the valley the train passed, puffing on the upgrade, dense steam hanging over its length, and the play of flames reflected from its engine cab.

For nearly a week the water ran colder, slower, clearer. On the first evening of December the wind went round to the west, the water became warmer, and fish became active. Gralaks was now ready to lay her eggs. Nearly five thousand were in the cavity beside her shrunken stomach. Spawning began towards the end of the night. During the darkness Salar had been roving round the pools, swimming from

Fireplay down the run into Wheel, questing under the ledge of rock and hollows under the bank of alders. But always he had returned in haste, to move behind the trough where Gralaks lay, beside one or another of his waiting rivals. Both pools were astir with restless fish.

At last the tail of Gralaks began to work more quickly, and immediately one of the cock-fish moved up beside her and shouldered her from the pit she had dug. Grai the parr pressed himself beside a large flat yellow stone which had been exposed by the digging. So tiny was Grai, that the cock-fish did not even know he was there. Thrust off the redd, Gralaks swam forward her own length, and lay still, while Salar moved in beside the cock-fish. Immediately this fish turned with a sweep of its porpoise-bitten tail and came at Salar with open mouth. Salar swung round to avoid the lunge and also to grip his rival across the wrist. The swirl lifted Grai and scattered gravel. Grai recovered and darted to the trough again, to be behind the tail of Gralaks.

Heedless of the turmoil behind her, but thereby excited, Gralaks had turned on her right side, to bend head and body backwards until her belly was curved palely like a water-sunk reflection of the young moon. She jerked and shook on her side, as though trying to touch the back of her neck with her tail. Eggs dribbled quickly from her, sinking with the current amidst gravel and sand and rolling into the trough.

The sight of the eggs and the taste of the water made Salar quiver; and as Gralaks moved backwards he moved forward, feeling as though he were being drawn from underneath by a lamprey of sweeter and sweeter sensation. His milt flowed from him in a mist, millions of invisible organisms wriggling in the water. Some of them found eggs, into the skins of which they bored, desperate for security. Those which were successful in finding the liquid within were lost in the creation of new life; the rest drifted away, to perish in water palely lighted by the star-galaxy of night, whose mirrored fate was their own.

For a few moments Salar lay in ecstasy on the redd, but his larger rival seized him by the tail and held him despite his violent lashings. Salar's head swung downstream; water was opening his gills, he could not breathe. The big fish swam upstream to drown him. The water was beaten and the two bodies rolled over. The other fish which was attending Gralaks was a grilse of her own school, which she had led from the Island Race; and this fish, whose back was a marbled pattern of green and pink, followed the struggle and in his excitement bit the larger salmon across the tail. This made it lose its hold of Salar, and dash downstream after the male grilse, abandon the chase, and swing up again below the redd and lie there. Salar returned more slowly and lay behind it, and to one side. The grilse also returned, and the three fish lay there, at rest for the moment.

During the struggle and chase, Gralaks had laid again, and Grai had covered the eggs. He lay beside Gralaks, by her right pectoral fin which was wider than his own width. He was fatigued. Unknowingly he had given fertility to nine of the two hundred and thirty eggs which had trickled from Gralaks like a necklace of small amber beads strung on water.

After a rest Grai moved away to the shelter of a stone. From the stone he moved to his lie under the bank, his spawning done for that year. Most of his milt had been lost six weeks before, when he had been caught on an artificial fly during the last day of the fishing season. The angler had held Grai in his hand, and the touch of unwetted palm and fingers had been a scalding agony to the little fish writhing to escape. The fisherman had held the parr after he had worked the barb of the hook from the corner of Grai's mouth, to illustrate to his son carrying the net the difference in strength between a small trout and a parr of equal size and almost equal appearance. Holding Grai in his fist, he told the boy to observe the muscular strength. It was during that agony that Grai had shed most of his milt. It wetted the angler's hand, a chalk-white liquid, after the parr's release. That was in October; now it was three weeks before Christmas.

During the day following his first spawning, Grai rested himself; but the next night he was back again at the redd, lying behind the three great fish of whom now he was wary and afraid. But when Garroo the cannibal trout moved up beside him, Grai left the Fireplay and went down to other redds below the Wheel Pool and the yew-trees and waited behind a pair of sea-trout spawning in fast water there. Grai was hungry. Scores of eggs he swallowed as they rolled down between the stones.

All the other parr and trout of the river were feeding on eggs, too. Biggest of the berry-gatherers, as Shiner called them, was Garroo. Salar drove him many times from the redd of Gralaks. Shiner used to climb an alder beside the Fireplay Pool, and in the clear water of sunlit noon he saw the fish there. Gralaks was almost hidden in the blur of the deeper water; behind her lay Salar, his red coat looking browny-purple under water, then the larger and darker fish, with the bite out of its tail-fin, and the smaller form of the male grilse. Behind the trio of square tails lay a big-headed black fish which was Garroo.

When the two larger cock-fish turned inwards to menace one another, Shiner knew the hen-fish was about to lay again. While the two big salmon were chasing and counter-chasing, the smaller fish moved up on to the redd; and at the same time Garroo thrust forward and turned on his side to suck the eggs into his mouth. Then the grilse would chase Garroo away, and move up again to the redd. But Salar or the other cock-fish, whichever returned first, drove the grilse off, and followed him downstream, while Garroo fled before the grilse. Shiner would see the waves of pursuit going round the bend.

A few moments later they would come back. The wan winter sunlight revealed every white and yellow and brown stone of the gravel over which Salar moved. Just behind him was the male grilse, and just behind the grilse was Garroo, his black jaw, scarred and misshapen, protruding as though with a leer at all such foolishness as spawning. Garroo's milt glands had long since shrunken in wicked old age.

A fortnight before Christmas the weather became cold again. The river was running low, many of its feeders on the moor being fringed with ice. The larger cock-fish with the bitten tail could no longer get on to the redd. Salar had to go past the stones and drift down to settle in the trough by the side of Gralaks. Even then his back and tail-fin were out of water. While he was coming back tail-first, the smaller grilse usually slithered over the heaped gravel and bit him across the wrist. Salar slashed the grilse away, and the movement scattered some of the eggs, which Garroo caught on the end of his kype. Shiner, watching from the tree, heard a distinct snapping noise as each egg was sucked into the trout's mouth.

Another time Shiner saw Salar chase Garroo round the pool, down the run into the Wheel Pool, and up again to the Fireplay, where the salmon caught the trout across the back and shook it, his head out of water. "'Twas just like a terrier shaking an ould black rat," said Shiner.

As the days went on Salar became heavy with weariness. Most of his milt was shed; in slow pulse after slow pulse his life's sweetness had been drawn from him, leaving with each emptiness a greater inflaming desire, which during the day lapped about the wasted body with dreams of an everlasting sea of rest; but when darkness came, and the water was ashine with stars, he felt himself running bright with the river, and sweetness returned to him on the redd beside Gralaks.

The time came when the last of the eggs were spawned, and

Gralaks was gone, dropping back to the Wheel Pool, where Trutta was lying.

Trutta was dark brown, and thin. He had fought to cover the eggs of a clove-spotted sea-trout, a handsome hen-fish nearly as long as himself, but slimmer and younger, most pleasant to see and be near to; yet no milt had come from him. He had driven away all other sea-trout; and had it not been for the little peal which were ever ready to shed their milt, none of the eggs of that female would have hatched ninety days later.

Trutta remained on guard, never sleeping; and no salmon, even the forty-three-pounder who had arrived, a clean-run fish, in the last week of December, was allowed to approach his mate—as Trutta considered her. The hen-fish laid her eggs, indifferent to the clashes about her: the nearness of the little peal, with their dark mother-of-pearl hues, gave her contentment.

When the last egg was gone from her, hidden under the stones of the redd, she drifted down the river, and came to the shelter of the alder roots above Humpy Bridge.

She lay there, day after day, night after night, waiting for the rain and the spate which would take her down to the sea. Near her lay Gralaks. Kelt and graveling rested side by side, thin, discoloured, empty of all feeling, patiently awaiting the rain.

25 *End and Beginning*

The colder the water, the greater its density. In the frosty nights of the year's end fish sank close to the rock and gravel of the pools, hardly moving. Those late-running salmon which had paired, and had not yet spawned, lay side by side in the fast water, which hid them although their back-fins were above a broken and uneven surface. The fever smouldered in them, as they waited for the frost to go.

Sticks and ferns near the waterfalls and fast glides around rocks which were wetted by spray slowly became coated with ice. Under many of the alders long stems of brambles were trailing in the water. These were cadets of the main root which during the past summer had set out to make their own lives. The exploring heads had put forth roots on finding water; these roots were spread long and white on the surface. As the water lipped them, so frost made a layer of ice on them. Soon the brambles were stretched straight, downstream, with a weight of ice on the ineffectual roots. When the ice-club became too heavy, the bramble broke and was dragged away. Ice began to dull the sight of the river where it was least alive: at the edges of pools and by the bays in the bank trodden by cattle. The frost had brought down the last leaves of waterside trees, and these had caught, one behind another, against outstanding stones of the shallows. The waterflow pressed them together in the shape of fir-cones, scores and even hundreds of leaves wadded together, and beginning to decompose on their undersides. This gave a little warmth, which was sought by snails and shrimps. Frost put its blind grey seal around the cones of leaves; frost bound together the roots of rushes; frost sealed the trickling places of the river, and thickened the icicles under the falls. Water found new trickling places; these too were sealed. Rocks and snags lipped by water were given brittle grey collars, which became wider until they broke off and floated into eddies and were welded into the local ice, strengthening it.

The slow solidification of eddies and still stretches by the shallows made the runs faster. New eddies were formed in reaction, new ice affirmed their stillness.

Towards noon the sun in a clear sky melted the rime on bracken and grasses, and in the straying hoofmarks of cattle and deer. Some of the grey sheets of ice cracked, and were borne down, making the water colder. No fly hatched, no fish moved. The larger eels were in the Atlantic, journeying under the Gulf Stream, seeking by instinct the weed-beds of the Sargasso. Smaller eels, the survivors of which would set forth the next autumn, were torpescent in holes and under stones. A large sheet of ice covering the stiller water of the Wheel Pool suddenly whimpered and cracked and tilted, then settled again on the slowly turning water.

The little heat of the sun was soon lost in a frost of gold and lengthening shadows. Ice floes which had stopped by the piers of Humpy Bridge were sealed to the stonework. The sun went down behind the trees, grass drooped again as rime grew white on its blades. Thin layers of water stroked the floes, thickening them. Gralaks lay in the deepest water, never moving.

Up in the Fireplay Pool Salar lay below the redd, as though guarding it. Clots of semi-opaque, jelly-like water passed him: a slush of ice. Rapidly within his body the germs of salmon-pest were multiplying; and as they conquered the living tissue weakened by the long strain of waiting stagnant in the river, so the vegetable fungus strengthened its hold on that tissue. Other forms of life were claiming that which in Salar had been assembled and used for a racial purpose of which he knew nothing. Salar was nearly emptied of self. He lay behind the redd, awaiting the rhythm of desire and all pleasure, seeing the stars wavery bright as he had seen them in the lustihood of Atlantic nights.

The fungus grew rapidly in the cold water. Soon Salar's jaw was covered with cream-coloured ruffs. The edges and centre of his tail-fin were corroded, too, and his skin, which had thickened and caused the scales to shrink since his return from the sea, was also patched with fungus where it had been bruised on the weirs, and by fighting.

One night when the Fireplay was covered with ice except for a narrow canal Salar saw many fish moving before him. One of them was Gralaks, leaping with silver coat, and returning to lie beside him. Salar drove at the other fish, for they would lure Gralaks from him. They fled from him, and vanished beyond the redd. Gralaks moved to the redd, and grew larger, until she was all the river which was streaming with stars along her flanks: she covered Salar, and was the river in spate and all the shining strength of ocean. But the fish came back, and were black, opening monstrous grampus-mouths to crush him, and Salar fled down the river which now was all broken water to bruise him and a weir which was high as the stars. The weir was a flood of red water, and thundering about him; then it was gone, and he saw the redd before him.

It was a goods train passing over the viaduct.

Salar had hardly moved, except to roll over in the delirium of his sickness.

The ice began to thaw the next day, with the coming of the south-west wind. Its melting released oxygen into the water, and Salar was stimulated to leap from the pool, falling back in a formless splash. Shiner saw the leap: he saw the lean rusty-brown body, the prolonged misshapen head covered with creamy fungus, green slime on the gill-covers and the blackened jaw with its great white hook twisted and tipped with yellow. Edges of all the fins were yellow, too, while a rosette was fixed to the side, spreading out from the scar of the lamprey-wound.

"Poor old chap," said Shiner. "What you needs now is a nice li'l fresh, to take you down to the sea, to clean yourself."

The south-west was blowing, but it brought no rain. By the beginning of February the river was at low summer level again. The phantom of spent passion for which Salar had remained by the redd was gone from him; he lay now in the deeper Wheel Pool, under the shelf of rock beside Trutta. At night the two kelts moved up to the edge of the run where it broke over the shallow. Warmer water had delayed the growth of fungus, but the pest bacillus had spread through his body, heart, liver, and gut. Strips of his skin, which fungus had covered, had broken away, and the spent body had no strength for regrowth.

In the still deeps of the pool a dim blue-grey length lay, the rival of Salar. Two more dead cock-fish lay on their backs in the Fireplay. They had died while waiting by redds in the shallows above, and the stream had brought them down. Every pool in the Two Rivers held dead or dying male fish. The wind was now from the north-east, a barren wind of drouth, a dry cutting wind which made lambs on the moor huddle into their ewes, and drove all birds into the lower valleys and the estuary.

When Shiner next saw Salar the kelt was lying at the edge of the Fireplay, in still water, over a silt of mud and buried sticks. Salar did not move as Shiner knelt down and stared at him. He did not see the man above him. Even when Shiner put a hand out and curved it under the kelt's body, as though to support it, there was no movement. Only when he lifted it did Salar come back from his farawayness of self, and feel a shock, and move off slowly into deep water.

"You mustn't bide by the bank, midear," said Shiner. "That ould crane ban't like Shiner, you know. He'll give 'ee a dapp that won't do no one no good." Old Nog, passing in the sky, uttered a screech. "You bestways must wait where you be now, until the rain cometh, midear." The pale mask in the water moved forward. "That's right, midear. Shiner knoweth." And talking to himself, the old man ambled away along the river bank, peering into the water, seeing almost everything that happened.

Night after night was starless. Clouds passed over the valley from the west, driven by a high salt wind which ruffled the pools and scattered the packs of leaves on stones of the shallows. Plants of hornwort and celery began to spread on the gravel their first leaves of the year, and the crowsfoot was lengthening green near them. The dipper sang its soliloquy of stones-and-water; the kingfisher lanced its cry under the leafless alders. On the top of a spruce higher than the railway viaduct a missel-thrush sang to the flaming purple sunset.

With the last of the winter's night, snow began to fall on the moor, moulding itself thinly on the windward side of writhen beeches and thorns, falling thin and pale and shrinking to beads of water, but always falling, until the black places where turf had been cut were white, and clumps of moor-grass were cowled in white with flakes falling thicker until all save water was white. In the morning it was a new world upon which the sun looked briefly before clouds hid it again in snow with which the wind whitely streamlined all things standing from the earth—pillars of the viaduct, trunks of trees, felled timber, ploughshare left in an unfinished furrow, abandoned motor-cars, and sheep huddled under the hedges. Through the snow the otters romped, making a slide down the cattle-break in the bank of the yew-trees, whose portent dark loomed through night's glimmer.

When the moon rose in a clear sky the otters remained by their slide of trodden snow, sliding together and singly, violently and easily, into the water, whistling and talking and wrostling and splashing until sharp heads pointed up the pool, to the noise of a jumping fish. Salar had leapt, the second time in the New Year. A wild hope of a spate and the sea had stirred in him. Together the otters slipped into the water.

Trutta lay beside Salar. Wherever Salar had gone during the past month, Trutta had gone too, following the phosphoric gleam of the kelt's head and flank and tail. When Salar saw the swimming shapes of otters above him, he went wildly away downstream; but Trutta, sure of the deep water, turned with open mouth and swam up hard and bumped the larger otter. Then Trutta, his mouth still open, swam down and swam up again to bump the other otter. He did this again and again, followed them round the pool. Shiner was hidden behind the oak-tree, and saw what happened. The big pug bumped the otters again and again, until they were growling with rage and one of them ran out on the bank, standing up on its hind-legs and "chittering". Then it either saw or smelled Shiner, for after that he neither heard nor saw them more.

But when Shiner returned the next day he saw, lying on the gravel edge above the Fireplay, lapped by rising coloured water of the thaw, a great head with twisted kype joined to a backbone from

Michael J. Loates

which the flesh had been stripped, and a large tail-fin frayed convex at the edges. The otters had returned, and driven Trutta into thin water where he was helpless; and when they had killed and left him, a fox, who while passing over the viaduct had heard the noises of splashing and growling, had crept down to the river with his vixen.

And a hundred yards below the Fireplay Shiner found a kelt with fungus on its head and tail and flank, lying on its side in water not deep enough to cover it. Salar had got so far with the last of his strength, and had died in the darkness.

The spate rose rapidly and washed all away, to the sea which gives absolution alike to the living and the dead.

In the gravel of the moorland stream the eggs were hatching, little fish breaking from confining skins to seek life, each one alone, save for the friend of all, the Spirit of the waters. And the star-stream of heaven flowed westward, to far beyond the ocean where salmon, moving from the deep water to the shallows of the islands, leapt— eager for immortality.

Michael J. Loates.

HERE ends *Salar the Salmon* by Henry Williamson,
begun in January 1935 at Shallowford and finished
in August 1935 in the field below Windwhistle
Spinney in Devon.